THIS DOCUME  G GROUP ORGANIZED BY)F CALIFORNIA, AT B /ERSITY, IN ST. LOUIS.

AUTHORS:

Franz Schurmann, Chairman of the Center for Chinese Studies; Peter Dale Scott, Department of English; Reginald Zelnik, Department of History; of the University of California at Berkeley.

CONSULTANTS:

Robert Browne, Department of Economics, Fairleigh-Dickinson University; George McT. Kahin, Department of Government, Cornell University; Daniel Lev, Department of Political Science, Joseph R. Levenson, Department of History, Carl E. Schorske, Department of History, University of California, Berkeley; Stanley Spector, Asian Studies, Washington University, St. Louis.

EDITORIAL:

Robert Buckhout, Richard Hazelton, Lindsay Mattison, and Jerome Schiller, Washington University, St. Louis; Frederick Crews, University of California, Berkeley; Gloria Commoner and Linda Mattison.

A CITIZENS' WHITE PAPER

A Study of United States Responses
to Pressures for a Political Settlement
of the Vietnam War: November 1963 - July 1966

THE POLITICS OF ESCALATION IN VIETNAM

by Franz Schurmann, Peter Dale Scott,
Reginald Zelnik

WITH A FOREWORD BY
ARTHUR SCHLESINGER, JR.

Summary and Conclusions by Carl E. Schorske

A FAWCETT PREMIER BOOK
Fawcett Publications, Inc., Greenwich, Conn.
Member of American Book Publishers Council, Inc.

A hardcover edition of this book is available from Beacon Press.

Library of Congress Catalog Card Number: 66-28916

First Fawcett Premier printing, October 1966

Published by Fawcett World Library,
67 West 44th Street
New York, New York 10036

Printed in the United States of America

Contents

This is the established order of Things, when a Nation has grown to such an height of Power as to become dangerous to Mankind, she never fails to loose her Wisdom, her Justice and her Moderation, and with these she never fails to loose her Power; which however returns again, if those Virtues return.

John Adams
1778, Autobiography, *Vol 4, page 158*

Foreword

This does not pretend to be a work of history: it is too soon to expect an authoritative account of the evolution of American policy toward Vietnam. It is rather a careful analysis, executed by disinterested scholars and based necessarily on public sources, of critical stages in the development of this policy. The questions raised by this analysis are questions that historians must answer some day—and which, in a democracy, policy-makers should answer now.

The fundamental issue implied in *The Politics of Escalation in Vietnam* is whether our government really wishes a political settlement in Southeast Asia, or whether its dominating, if still unavowed, goal has not imperceptibly become an illusory military "victory." After a close examination of the relationship between diplomatic and military action in Vietnam in the years since the overthrow of Diem, the authors believe they have found a pattern in United States policy. The chief American moves to widen the war, they contend, seem to have come at times of particular pressure for negotiation; and our own gestures toward negotiation seem to have preceded, or even cloaked, steps toward our larger military involvement. Their conclusion is that our government has appeared to regard the possibility of a negotiated solution more as a threat than as a promise.

The authors do not claim that their analysis proves these propositions. They are aware of the limitations of their evidence and recognize that, until the diplomatic files are opened, their suspicions cannot be concluded one way or the other. I would also say that they do not, in my judgment, give due weight to the military necessities that may at times have rendered an enlarged American role imperative; nor do they always see that negotiation gestures out of Hanoi can be exercises in political warfare too; nor can one in all cases share their assessment of particular situations.

But, whatever its limitations, the analysis does make points of the utmost importance. It shows, for example, that the diplomatic record is a good deal more complicated than our highest government officials have led us to believe—that the other side, far from systematically rebuffing a series of "unconditional" American overtures, has from time to time, despite the pressure to continue the war steadily emanating from Peking, betrayed flickers of interest in a political settlement that a vigorous and imaginative American diplomacy would surely have exploited, if only to establish our goodwill before the world. The analysis suggests too how the momentum generated by the extraordinary American military presence in Vietnam has begun to overwhelm diplomatic considerations, producing an illusion in Washington that military means can solve an essentially political problem and that, in any case, military considerations must have first priority.

Historians may finally determine that the thesis of *The Politics of Escalation in Vietnam* is wrong. In the meantime, the questions it raises are legitimate and searching. One would hope that they might now elicit authoritative answers —and that the response might be set forth, not in stale official rhetoric about Chinese expansionism, the Munich analogy, molesting neighbors, fighting for freedom and so on, but in the sober and responsible factuality to which citizens of a democracy are entitled from their leaders.

ARTHUR SCHLESINGER, JR.

Authors' Note

JUNE 26, 1966

The turbulent rush of events in a mounting crisis of national destiny so momentous as the war which engages the United States in Vietnam makes it difficult for even the best-informed individual to maintain a clear sense of direction. This is as true for policy-makers compelled to respond to rapidly changing situations as for responsible citizens and scholars seeking to exercise an informed judgment on the actions of their leaders. Each is absorbed by the pressing claims of the immediate situation at the expense of his awareness of the larger trends.

The war in Vietnam has taught us that our nation has an urgent need to consider its recent experience in a larger perspective. The Great Debate concerning our involvement and our goals, enlightening as it has been, has not been informed by a secure sense of the patterns emerging from recent events. Accordingly, we offer this examination of the record with the specific purpose of defining one of these patterns.

Our purpose here is to describe significant American moves toward expansion and intensification of the war within the context of relevant political events, both Vietnamese and international, and by so doing to call public attention to the questionable relationship between American acts of escalation and specific initiatives by others for peaceful settlement of the conflict.

While we are acutely aware that we do not command all the evidence to construct a full and balanced picture of policy formation or its consequences, we hope that our construction, based on facts in the public record, will induce our political leaders either to correct our version where it may be in error, or, if it be found accurate, as we believe it is, to answer to its implications regarding United States policy. For the consequences of intensified warfare as a recurrent American response in a context of pressures for political accommodation have become sufficiently grave to call for a searching reassessment of U. S. policy.

The attached report contains studies of nine critical periods in the Vietnam war. In each of these periods the pattern of U. S. military escalation in the context of Vietnamese or international pressures for negotiations is shown to persist, despite the special character of each episode. Although in the first two of these periods military involvement is less prominent than in the later periods, all serve as background for an understanding of the Administration's proclivity to see as threat rather than as promise the emergence of Vietnamese or neutral initiatives for compromise political solutions. The effect of the American actions has been not merely to deepen our military commitment but also to weaken the credibility of United States government officials who publicly claim that they are searching for a real basis for negotiations.

Summary and Conclusions

Three major factors have affected the increasingly critical course of the Vietnam war: the indigenous politics of South Vietnam, the international pressures for a negotiated settlement, and the military actions of the belligerents. An examination of the interrelation of these factors in nine critical periods, beginning with the fall of Ngo Dinh Diem in November 1963, reveals a recurrent pattern. Movements toward a political settlement have been retarded or broken off by American interventions, most of which have taken the form of military escalation.

Available evidence does not prove that escalations were intended solely or primarily to counter efforts at compromise or negotiation. A study of the chronology of American escalations within the political context reveals, however, that the major American intensifications of the war have been preceded less by substantially increased military opposition than by periods of mounting pressure for a political settlement of the war.

The case studies presented here document a recurrent pattern in situations varying in their historical character. Sometimes overtures of pressures toward compromise solutions have emanated from political elements in South Vietnam or North Vietnam, sometimes from international powers. There have been repeated waves of Buddhist agitation against the South Vietnamese military dictatorship. These have inevitably extended into agitation for peace, since the war and the military dictatorship have been used to justify and reinforce each other. The United States has become equally identified with both as repeated indigenous efforts to liberalize the regime have raised the issue of a compromise settlement as the logical corollary of political self-determination. (See especially Sections II and IV.)

Particularly during 1964, and again at the turn of the year 1966, efforts toward a negotiated settlement have emanated from international sources. The initiatives of President de Gaulle, Secretary-General U Thant, the Soviet Union, Yugoslavia, and Canada are notable among the repeated attempts, all of which were fruitless, to bring the belligerents to the conference table. Finally, there were initiatives from the National Liberation Front (Vietcong) and from Hanoi, as well as collaborations of either or both of these with nonbelligerent initiatives, which likewise collapsed under United States escalation. (See Sections II and III.)

The most disturbing finding of this study is thus the pattern in which moves toward political settlement are brought to a close with an intensification of the war by the United States. Even allowing for exclusively military considerations as motivating United States escalation, their repeated impact upon encouraging prospects of political solutions justifies the gravest concern. Should the pattern persist, escalations will continue to reduce the possibilities of a realistic political alternative to total victory, even while the United States professes its will to find one.

Military response to the peace moves of others has not been, of course, the only constituent in United States policy, though it has overshadowed its more promising concomitant —the search for a negotiated settlement. Yet even official efforts of the United States in this direction, as some of the case investigations show, have been terminated or disrupted by sudden United States military intrusions into the diplomatic process. (See Sections VI and IX.)

Despite the massive and accelerating increase in American military operations over the past two years, the salient speeches and public diplomatic positions taken by both sides in the war suggest a pattern of movement, however uneven, toward a common basis for political solutions. At first, it was the Communists who tried to press for political discussions, often with neutral or United Nations encouragement. (January and July, 1964; February-March 1965; see Sections II, III, and IV.) Since President Johnson's Baltimore speech of April 7, 1965, however, the United States has appeared more committed to the search for a negotiated solution than before, while its opponents have tended to place more demanding conditions in the way of negotiations. (See Sections V and VIII.) The President's Baltimore speech seemed indeed like a turning point. Only a month before, Secretary of

State Rusk had repeated his oft-stated position that "we are not going to negotiate to reward aggression" (TV interview, March 7, 1965). The Rusk doctrine of the "missing piece" asserted that no negotiations could be considered until some guarantee existed that Hanoi was "prepared to stop doing what it is doing against its neighbors" (Press conference, February 25, 1965). President Johnson, in his Baltimore speech, seemed to alter this doctrine when he called for "unconditional discussions." By December 1965, the position of the United States was more explicitly accommodating to the Geneva-oriented position of the other side and important neutrals. Secretary Rusk proclaimed his unconditional willingness to "go to Geneva tomorrow." Finally, in its "fourteen points" of January 1966 (Appendix A), the United States unequivocally accepted the possibility of peace on the "basis" of the Geneva Agreements of 1954 and 1962. Free elections in South Vietnam and the eventuality of reunification were now included in the American diplomatic perspective.

While the publicly stated attitude of the United States toward a negotiated settlement became more flexible, the North Vietnamese appeared to grow more intransigent. In late 1964, as we now know, Hanoi accepted U Thant's idea of a secret diplomatic meeting, which the United States rejected. On April 8, 1965, at about the time of President Johnson's Baltimore speech, Premier Pham Van Dong of the Democratic Republic of Vietnam presented his "four points." They reiterated the specific demands of the 1954 Agreements for withdrawal of foreign troops and neutralization of the "two zones" during a temporary division, to be followed by "peaceful reunification" without foreign interference. The internal affairs of South Vietnam were to be settled "in accordance with the program of the South Vietnam National Front for Liberation." The Premier claimed that his four points were the "basis for the soundest political settlement of the Vietnam problem," adding that "if this basis is recognized," an international Geneva-type conference could possibly be reconvened. Although these four points have remained the negotiating position of the North Vietnamese government, they have subsequently been presented in a more intransigent way. Specifically, the four points must now be "accepted," not merely "recognized," as a "basis" for negotiations. Furthermore, in accordance with the demands stated in the NLF "five points" of March 22, 1965, the National Liberation Front must be accepted as the "sole genuine representative" of the

South Vietnamese people. Though the use of the word "genuine" suggests that Hanoi might recognize other "representatives" of the South Vietnamese, the position of the North has accentuated differences from the United States, while the expression of the American diplomatic position has evolved toward a less uncompromising tone.

So far, we have examined these contrary diplomatic motions, turning about the speeches of April 7 and 8, only as they appear in the words of the two contenders. If we turn to the context of actions, however, the emergent pattern is one not of progress toward negotiation, but of graded escalation. And if we look more closely at the pattern of United States policy, one sees that it has been not changing but recurrent. For the Baltimore speech represents a turning point in our official rhetoric but not, closer analysis suggests, any turning point in United States policy. Even within the Baltimore speech, the President expressed the premises which have informed his policy before and since: that the Vietnam war is a case of external aggression, and that external aggression must never be appeased. The practical correlate of this policy is to find the road to peace by intensifying war. In the President's own words:

> The central lesson of our time is that the appetite of aggression is never satisfied. . . . We must say in Southeast Asia—as we did in Europe—in the words of the Bible: 'Hitherto shalt thou come, but no further.' Our objective is the independence of South Vietnam and its freedom from attack . . . We will do everything necessary to reach that objective. . . . In recent months attacks on South Vietnam were stepped up. Thus it became necessary for us to increase our response and to make attacks by air. This is not a change of purpose. . . . We do this in order to slow down aggression. . . . We will not be defeated. We will not grow tired. We will not withdraw, either openly or under the cloak of a meaningless agreement. We know that air attacks alone will not accomplish all of these purposes. But it is our best and prayerful judgment that they are a necessary part of the surest road to peace.

In the following memorandum, we have tried to show that the United States has placed its military policy of nullifying "aggression" ahead of a political means to a solution of the

Vietnam problem. The April 7, 1965, speech served as justification for the February 1965 escalation to the regular bombing of North Vietnam. It was also accompanied by press accounts which correctly predicted a significant increase in American troop commitments. More significant, President Johnson's speech came at a time when, in the words of *The New York Times,* "international pressures on the United States were growing to begin negotiating a settlement of the war" (*NYT,* April 2, 1965). The President addressed himself directly to three conditions which Western newspapers had (correctly) associated with the North Vietnamese terms for a peace conference. The United States had reportedly been asked to accept at least an eventual withdrawal of its troops, an eventual reunification of Vietnam, and an immediate cessation of air attacks on North Vietnam (*NYT,* April 1; London *Times,* April 1). The Baltimore speech rejected unambiguously all three of these conditions. The President's offer of "unconditional discussions" thus was made in a context of both rejection of the adversary's conditions for talks and of the first direct involvement of American troops in the ground war. In retrospect, escalation appears far more central to American purposes than the offer of "unconditional discussions," an offer almost certain to be rejected.

The case of the Baltimore speech, on its surface one of the clearest expressions of the American will to peace, dramatizes the pattern that we have explored in the following memorandum. *Like nearly all American escalation since the death of Ngo Dinh Diem,* the one which came in April followed chronologically upon a period of growing pressures for a political settlement, to which the President's speech replied. Sometimes these pressures for negotiations were prominent (as in this case, in March 1965) within the international community. Sometimes they emanated from the Saigon regime of the moment. Sometimes both international and local pressures developed at the same time.

In almost every case, such critical pressures for peace have issued in deepening United States commitment to the war in Vietnam. By the same token, each of the most dramatic escalations of the war by the United States has had the effect (if not the intention) of closing off such critical periods.

In the week of July 23, 1964, U Thant, President de Gaulle, and the Soviet government all called for a Geneva conference. In the week of August 2, the United States made its first overt attack on ships and territory of North Vietnam.

In January 1965, anti-American strikes and demonstrations in South Vietnamese cities and the displacement of Chinese by presumably more moderate Soviet influence in Hanoi were followed by the beginning of United States air bombardment of North Vietnam on February 7.

Efforts of Italian intermediaries La Pira and Fanfani in November and December of 1965 were followed on December 15 by the first bombing of the Haiphong area, which the Administration had been told would close the door to negotiations.

Even the disturbing pattern, of which other examples will be given in the following chronological survey, would not justify a simple argument for an inevitable causal connection between peace-making efforts of others and escalation by the United States. The peace missions of Ambassador Harriman in July 1965, and the travels of Senator Mansfield and his colleagues must stand as genuine political attempts by the United States to break out of the military impasse. Yet the record would suggest that militant counsels have generally prevailed in Washington. They will undoubtedly do so as long as the simple political model of Munich continues to exercise its false analogical magic over the minds of our policy-makers. The widening of war seems to remain a consistently favored alternative to a serious political approach to disengagement. This is apparently true even when United States efforts have elicited from the other side their pre-conditions for such disengagement, such as the recognition of the NLF as a negotiating party, or a cessation of bombing.

The somber, recurring pattern of political exploration cut short by military escalation, until it is either altered or disproved, thus remains more significant than recent changes in the belligerents' announced negotiating positions. Seen as the concrete experience of the other side, it may also explain why United States peace initiatives have no longer been met by a corresponding interest. Secretary Rusk's hollow one-week peace ultimatum of May 1965 offers a graphic instance of America's harsh combination of political and military practice. Similar episodes during the years 1964 and 1965, with massive American escalations, produced that widespread skepticism with which our overtures of peace have been greeted, not only in Hanoi but elsewhere throughout the world. We do not wish to subscribe to Ho Chi Minh's description of these overtures as a "trick," but the military conduct which accompanied them reveals deficiencies in the United States position which must be understood. Only through such an understanding can we as American citizens discern the true conditions of peace and the obstacles to its restoration.

I

Fall of Diem
(Late 1963)

SUMMARY: During the late summer and fall of 1963, the government of Ngo Dinh Diem, faced with increasing political unrest, resorted to increasingly severe repressive measures. Saigon's war effort languished as government officials devoted their attention to their own political survival. American disenchantment with Diem's performance led to gradual withdrawal of U.S. support of his rule. De Gaulle's proposal for a reunified Vietnam independent of "external influences" and concern in Washington over rumors that Diem's brother and advisor Nhu was exploring chances of a neutralist settlement with the Communists further strained U.S. patience. Finally, the United States, calling for a greater war effort, accepted complicity in the coup which ousted Diem.

Although the major concern of this report is with periods of escalation, it is helpful to look at two earlier critical periods when political upheaval in South Vietnam, manifested in street demonstrations and in intrigue in government circles, presented Washington with the real possibility of a political settlement of the war. Each time Washington reacted as though it were faced with a threat rather than an opportunity. The first such period was in 1963, when political unrest culminated in the military coup of November 1, resulting in the assassination of Premier Ngo Dinh Diem and his brother and "political adviser," Ngo Dinh Nhu. At that time, Washington revealed its tactics and intentions with unusual candor. *New York Times* correspondent Max Frankel reported:

> The Administration welcomes the coup d'etat in South Vietnam, assumes that its policies helped to bring it about and is confident of *greater progress now in the war against the Communist guerrillas.* . . . It is conceded here that the United States Government had created the atmosphere that made the coup possible (*NYT*, November 2, 1963, p. 1; emphasis added).

During the summer prior to the coup, there had been three and a half months of Buddhist street demonstrations. Retrospectively, it has been suggested that it was these demonstrations and American sympathy for them that led to the coup. News reports of the time tell a different story. The Buddhist demonstrations had effectively been cut off on August 21, 1963, by the repressive raid of Vietnamese Special Forces (in U.S. pay). Thus it was not the demonstrations that triggered the coup; rather, the moving cause seems to have been the announcement by the U.S. Embassy in Saigon on October 21 that United States pay for the South Vietnamese Special Forces would be terminated unless these Forces were employed in the field against the Communists (*NYT*, October 22, 1963, p. 1). Under this U.S. pressure, Diem and Nhu were reluctantly compelled to send their Special Forces out of the capital on October 30; left without their elite guard, the brothers fell within hours.

At the time of the U.S. announcement, it was also revealed that the United States had suggested to President Diem that "the war effort might be improved if Ngo Dinh Nhu left the Government" (*NYT*, October 22, 1963, p. 18). Two stories from Washington in a later issue of *The New York Times* make clear what probably motivated the Administration:

> President de Gaulle said last August 29 that France would cooperate with the people of Vietnam in an effort to unify the divided country and make it independent of 'external influences'. . . . Since then there has been a neutralist movement in Vietnam (*NYT*, January 30, 1964, p. 1).
>
> In Saigon, the French leader's offer was understood to have been received quite favorably by Ngo Dinh Nhu,

> brother and political adviser of then President Ngo Dinh Diem. . . . When the regime of President Diem was ousted in a coup on November 1 and 2, *the possibility of South Vietnam voluntarily accepting neutralism appeared to have been eliminated* (*NYT*, January 30, 1964, p. 2; emphasis added).

Since then it has been frequently suggested that Nhu "had begun some tentative talks with the guerillas in the South, if not actually with the leadership in the North." [1]

It is much less clear that Nhu was actually close to a settlement with the Communists, however, than that certain elements in Washington were alarmed by this danger (*New York Herald Tribune*, September 18, 1963). We are not suggesting that U.S. misgivings about neutralism were the sole or even the major contributing factor in the U.S. policy decisions which led to Diem's overthrow. On the contrary, Diem's regime seemed to be generally demoralized both at home and in the field. There were undoubtedly many U.S. leaders who took the position attributed to Ambassador Lodge at this time that a more broadly based, majoritarian government in Saigon might engage the support of the rapidly growing Buddhist organizations, and thus lead to a more united and vigorous war effort. All of the facts may one day be known; news reports of this period make at least two of these facts clear. One is that Washington recognized the existence in Saigon of neutralist sentiments among governmental officials. The other is that the desirability of a more popular government in Saigon was subordinated, in rhetoric as in practice, to the desirability of a more vigorous war effort, rather than vice versa.

[1] Jean Lacouture, *Vietnam: Between Two Truces* (New York, 1966, p. 82). Other evidence of the neutralist "threat" and indirectly of U.S. concern with it can be seen in the departure from Saigon of the French Ambassador Roger Lalouette in September 1963 "after it was reported that he was acting as a go-between for North Vietnam and the government of President Ngo Dinh Diem" (*The New York Times*, January 23, 1964, p. 12).

II

Neutralism and the Khanh Coup (January 1964)

SUMMARY: In this section we shall try to show that there was indeed open disaffection with the war effort within the city of Saigon itself, even if the Catholic minority continued to campaign against the neutralist alternative. The French-trained members of the junta of Duong Van Minh, which briefly succeeded Diem, might well, if left in power, have sought a broader, more representative base than the militant Catholic minority. Fear of neutralism was, in fact, the ground later given by General Khanh as an excuse for his overthrow of Duong Van Minh on January 30, 1964. But the Minh junta had, in effect, been publicly told from its outset by Americans who helped them to power that "progress in the war," not progress in popularity, should be its prime objective. And it was now clear to all concerned in Saigon that Washington was capable of helping to topple a South Vietnamese regime when neutralist inclinations were suspected.

If fear of a neutralist settlement, of a "plot between Paris, Hanoi, and Nhu" (Lacouture, *op. cit.*, p. 83) preceded the coup of November 1963, and may well have been one of its causes, similar fear preceded the next coup, that by General Nguyen Khanh on January 30, 1964. Indeed, General Khanh justified his coup on this ground. In his first press conference, he attacked those members of the previous Duong Van Minh regime who "adopted a servile attitude, paving the way for neutralism and thus selling out the country" (FBIS *Daily*

Report, February 3, 1964, KKK1). He thus indirectly confirmed the earlier press reports of the coup:

> Reliable informants in Saigon said General Khanh had told Americans that the coup was intended to save South Vietnam from a neutral settlement like the one imposed in Laos in 1954. . . . The plot, he said, was to have coincided with France's recognition of Communist China, which was announced Tuesday (January 28) (*NYT,* January 30, 1964, p. 1).

> A Vietnamese source . . . said last night that two of the four generals arrested had been negotiating with the French for two weeks. . . . "We were anxious about them indeed," the source said, "and we had conclusive proof that they had been talking with the French in terms of a neutralized Vietnam and that North Vietnam had given support to the plan" (*NYT,* January 30, 1964, p. 3).

At the time, there was a tendency in Washington to discount this story, and also to voice regret that the Minh regime had been so quickly overthrown. Yet there is evidence, not all of it publicly known in the West at the time, to indicate that the risk of neutralization was real. We shall deal with this evidence by categories, inasmuch as a similar pattern of events will be seen to recur in subsequent "critical periods."

1. *International forces were working for neutralization.*

On January 27, General de Gaulle announced France's recognition of the Chinese Peoples Republic; and this major event was clearly related, in part at least, to the situation in Vietnam. As the Associated Press noted: "The French hope their move will restore their influence in the four countries which once comprised French Indo-China" (*San Francisco Chronicle,* January 28, 1964, p. 1). Confirmation came on January 31, when

> President de Gaulle . . . made it clear that the hope of neutralizing Southeast Asia—where France was once a colonial power—was one of the main reasons for establishing diplomatic relations with the Peking regime last Monday (*San Francisco Chronicle,* February 1, 1964, p. 1).

The Secretary-General of the United Nations, U Thant, was also encouraging the establishment of a coalition regime in South Vietnam, though this was not made public until much later:

> After the fall of the Ngo Dinh Diem Government in November, 1963, it was disclosed today, (U Thant) suggested to the United States that it promote a coalition government in Saigon that would include a number of non-Communist Vietnamese political exiles, especially those who had taken refuge in Paris. This would have brought in men who shared General de Gaulle's belief that South Vietnam must be neutralized (*NYT*, March 9, 1965, p. 4).

These overtures, as we shall see, were to have their sequel in Saigon.

2. *Communist forces were working for negotiations.*

The *Manchester Guardian* has reported, from "an unimpeachable source," that after the fall of Diem in late 1963, Hanoi "was willing to discuss the establishment of a coalition neutralist government in Saigon" (August 9, 1965).[1] On November 8, 1963, the clandestine radio of the National Liberation Front of South Vietnam ("Vietcong") broadcasted an appeal for the "opening of negotiations between various interested groups in South Vietnam, in order to arrive at a cease-fire and a solution to the great problems of the country."[2] The NLF also convened its Second Congress on

[1] Cf. U Thant on February 24, 1965: "In my view, there was a very good possibility in 1963 of arriving at a satisfactory political solution."

[2] According to Jean Lacouture (*Vietnam: Between Two Truces*, p. 170). The text of the broadcast in the CIA-sponsored FBIS *Daily Report*, which summarizes foreign broadcasts for the information of the U.S. State Department and other government agencies, does not contain this statement. FBIS files do contain, however, a similar appeal from the NLF to the Minh junta, after warning its members that they too might be dropped by the United States: "However, the coup promoters are still able to change what one calls their fate, and they still have enough time to replan their future—a future which will be brilliant, which will have no more nightmares—if they draw from the scenes of the ruins in Saigon a useful lesson, if they know how to rely on the people's strength to resolutely separate themselves from the

January 1, 1964; and on January 28, coinciding with the news of France's recognition of China, Hanoi Radio broadcast to South Vietnam the Appeal for Unity that had been promulgated by the NLF Congress. This Appeal for Unity was clearly addressed not only to the people of South Vietnam, but to their leaders:

> . . . to all forces . . . regardless of political view, religion, or race, regardless of their past, their present political and social position, or their political conflicts —to mobilize every capability to advance toward united actions and to seek the best solution of the situation in South Vietnam for the benefit of all Vietnamese people. . . . The National Liberation Front of South Vietnam asserted that *if the leaders of the South Vietnamese armed forces* are concerned with the people's happiness and future, they must consider that internal conflicts can be settled by means of negotiations (FBIS *Daily Report,* February 5, 1964, KKK2; Hanoi Radio Broadcast of January 28; emphasis added).

Although both of these broadcasts were translated and circulated by the Foreign Broadcast Information Service to the U.S. State Department, no notice of them appeared in the American press.

3. *There were pressures in Saigon for neutralization.*

General Khanh's denunciation of a neutralist-Gaullist plot within the junta of Duong Van Minh cannot be conclusively established with the available evidence. However, an analysis of the situation offered at the time by *Le Monde* seems plausible especially in the light of confirming evidence provided in the recent studies of Burchett and Lacouture.[3] According to this analysis, the issue that divided the basically moderate, pro-French Minh junta and the more militant, pro-

---

control of the U.S. Imperialists, if they are brave enough to rise up, and if they contribute their abilities to working for the fatherland, to achieving nation(al) independence, and to bringing freedom and democracy to the people. In so doing, they will not only preserve their reputation, but they will perform meritorious service for the country as well. Let them think it over" (FBIS *Daily Report,* November 13, 1963, KKK4).

[3] W. Burchett, *Vietnam: Inside Story of the Guerilla War* (New York, 1965), pp. 214-216; Jean Lacouture, *op. cit.,* pp. 120-133.

American Khanh was their degree of dedication to a resolute prosecution of the war. P Khanh, it is generally recognized, was very close at this time to the American commander Paul Harkins, and neither Harkins nor Khanh had been sympathetic to Washington's decision, in which Ambassador Lodge concurred, to dump Diem. According to *Le Monde*, Minh himself was in fact not neutralist, but had attempted to maintain a balanced position. He and his closer colleagues had adopted a strongly anti-French posture in public,

> . . . while striving to temporize, to avoid a rupture (with France), as demanded by some of their colleagues. One saw a proof of their moderation—or of their hesitation—in the fact that on many occasions anti-French demonstrations were followed by *counter-demonstrations favorable to neutralization* without the police having received orders to intervene (*LM*, February 1, 1964, p. 1; emphasis added).[4]

The fact that there were antiwar demonstrations at this time, as well as the publicized and officially organized anti-neutralist and anti-French demonstrations on December 20, January 13 and 18, was little known in the U.S. except to readers of *Le Monde* and a few other foreign journals. The Associated Press reported only that "student disorders . . . had widely varied aims" (*NYT*, January 18, 1964, p. 7).

The *Le Monde* reporter also noted that Minh had recalled from Paris Nguyen Van Vy, who was seen by many as a Trojan horse of neutralism, inasmuch as he was a leader of the pro-Gaullist exiles in France, on whom U Thant was relying for efforts toward negotiations.

The chief evidence of continuing neutralist pressures, however, was the ferocity with which neutralism was attacked. On January 26, for example,

> Premier Nguyen Ngoc Tho of South Vietnam said . . .

[4] Communist propaganda has always maintained that neutralist unrest was widespread, citing many specific instances. For example, according to Hanoi Radio: "All officers and men of the First Paratroop Battalion (Nguyen Trung Hieu barracks, in Hoi Hung, Saigon) said: 'We are fed up with the sight of Vietnamese killing Vietnamese. We are fed up with the war. We want peace. We are determined not to go on fighting.'" (FBIS *Daily Report*, February 7, 1964, JJJ4: Hanoi Radio, February 3.)

> that reported French plans to press for a negotiated settlement of the war were 'sabotaging us, killing us, drowning us in difficulties' (*NYT*, January 27, 1964).

On January 16, the government found it necessary to close down no fewer than nine Saigon newspapers (*NYT*, January 17, 1964, p. 2); the reason, according to Wilfred Burchett (*op. cit.*), was their having mentioned "the possibility of a neutralist solution." Throughout this period, the moderate and proneutralist Buddhist factions, led by Thich Tam Chau and Thich Tri Quang, respectively, encouraged by the overthrow of Diem, were consolidating and building a more powerful and effective movement (*NYT*, January 1, 1964, p. 2). At the same time, there were reports of unrest among the work forces in U.S. owned factories in and near Saigon, and at least one strike had to be put down bloodily.[5]

In short, it seems clear that disaffection with the war continued to manifest itself under the Minh junta, and that a militant general like Khanh could reasonably doubt the junta's capacity to respond, as the Americans were demanding, with a more vigorous prosecution of the war. This much evidence, at least, supports General Khanh's reported claim that his coup was a blow struck to forestall the threat of a political settlement.

4. *What was the role of the U.S. authorities?*

Jean Lacouture has recently argued that the Khanh coup can be attributed in part to the disappointment of the Americans with the Minh junta's prosecution of the war. Lacouture recalls particularly the disappointment

> of the officers on General Harkins' staff, who soon began to look for candidates and to sound out the malcontents. Two of these emerged above all the others: Generals Nguyen Khanh and Duong Van Duc. (Lacouture, *op. cit.*, p. 131)

[5] The NLF Clandestine Radio alleged that a strike of 2,000 at the Vinatexco mill had been put down with some 200 casualties (FBIS *Daily Report*, February 7, 1964, p. 7, KKK2). The estimate of casualties by the AP was "about 20 girls" (*NYT*, January 18, 1964, p. 7).

The U.S. press had noted the lack of trust and sympathy between Harkins and the junta, and had speculated that he might be replaced (*NYT*, January 15, 1964, p. 6). Other sources testify to the close personal relationship between Generals Khanh and Harkins at this time and to Harkins' alleged interest in the discovery of a new Vietnamese "strongman," at a time when Ambassador Lodge was exerting efforts to establish a civilian regime. One cannot from the available public evidence establish American complicity in the coup of January 30, 1964, the news of which (unlike that of November, 1963) was coolly received in Washington. Indeed, *Le Monde* reported at the time that the United States authorities,

> caught off balance (*débordés*) by Khanh's initiative, even if certain of their local agents did not discourage it (General Harkins is almost certainly meant here), regret the (new) era of instability (*LM*, February 1, 1964, p. 1).

Our purpose in this section is not to speculate on the precise degree of U.S. complicity or noncomplicity in the Khanh coup. That is a task for future historians. We wish rather to suggest that, precisely at a moment when neutralist sentiment was increasing in Saigon and elsewhere, the shift from a moderate to a militant government in Saigon was accompanied by a shift in Washington's declared policy from limited to unlimited support for the Vietnam war. It is important to recall, in this regard, the stated intention of the Kennedy administration, as announced by McNamara and Taylor from the White House on October 2, 1963, which was to withdraw most U.S. forces from South Vietnam by the end of 1965.[6] The first public indication of a change in the U.S. intentions came in a letter from President Johnson to Duong Van Minh at New Year's, 1964, which promised "the fullest measure of support . . . in achieving victory." *The New York Times* commented, "By implication, the message erased the previous date for withdrawing the bulk of

[6] Three weeks after the assassination, on December 19 and 20, 1963, McNamara and CIA chief John A. McCone visited Saigon to evaluate the war efforts of the new Saigon government. "McNamara told the junta leaders that the United States was prepared to help . . . as long as aid was needed" (*NYT*, January 2, 1964, p. 7).

United States forces from Vietnam by the end of 1965" (*NYT*, January 2, 1964, p. 7).[7] A more explicit official indication of reversal of policy came in the testimony of Secretary McNamara before the Armed Services Committee, on January 27, three days before the coup:

> The survival of an independent government in South Vietnam is so important to the security of Southeast Asia and to the free world that I can conceive of no alternative other than to take all necessary measures within our capability to prevent a Communist victory.[8]

Immediately after the coup, James Reston reported from Washington:

> We are probably coming to the end of the period when the United States would neither fight nor negotiate. And we are probably approaching a new phase when both fighting and negotiating will be stepped up (*NYT*, January 31, 1964, p. 26).

Military developments in 1964 were to confirm Reston's prediction with respect to the fighting, if not to negotiations. In retrospect, it is hard to deny that, shortly before the coup, the United States had made the crucial decision to reverse the policy, announced during the last days of President Kennedy's administration, of gradually withdrawing U.S. troops from South Vietnam. Was it all a coincidence that a change in leadership in Washington was followed by a change in policy, and a change in policy by a corresponding change in Saigon's government?[9] Administration officials have never yet seen fit to defend publicly this important re-

[7] The letter reportedly renounced unequivocally "any prospect for a neutralist solution for South Vietnam . . . at a time when neutralist sentiment has been gaining currency in some political and intellectual circles here" (in South Vietnam). (*NYT*, January 2, 1964.)

[8] M. Raskin and B. Fall, *The Vietnam Reader*, (New York, 1965), p. 394.

[9] Hanoi Radio on February 4 also saw in the coup evidence that "the United States had blotted out its decision to withdraw part of the United States troops from South Vietnam" (FBIS *Daily Report*, February 5, 1964, JJJ6).

versal of policy; thus they have not identified the threat that brought it about. Was it a radical increase in the strength of the opposing forces? As far as we know, none has ever been alleged. Or was it a radical decline in Saigon's will to resist, with a corresponding disposition toward the political proposals of de Gaulle and the NLF?

One conclusion can be asserted unequivocally: The United States increased its commitment to a prolongation of the Vietnam war at a time when the drift of the Saigon junta and of public opinion was in the direction of negotiations for a neutralized Vietnam. The threat of a serious divergence between Washington's interest in the war and Saigon's was temporarily postponed by the success of the January 30 coup.

III

Tonkin Gulf Incident (July—August 1964)

SUMMARY: The context of events that constitute the "Tonkin Gulf incident" of August 2 and 4, 1964, remains to this day unclear; conflicting accounts of actions and their causes, contradictory versions of the sequence of events, allegation and counterallegation obscure the history of these momentous days, and only the outcome is beyond doubt. For the direct result of the minor naval action in Tonkin Gulf in the early days of August was the bombardment of North Vietnam by U.S. aircraft on August 5, 1965. This bombardment, the first overt American attack on the North, marked a new phase in U.S. "commitment" in Vietnam, and a further stage in U.S. escalation of the war.

Though the record of the incidents in Tonkin Gulf is incomplete, enough facts are available concerning both the action there and the Vietnamese situation at large to permit intelligent speculation on the reasons for the sudden American bombing of the North. Careful study of these facts suggests that the U.S. attack on the North was no simple act of "reprisal" for an alleged North Vietnamese naval offensive in Tonkin Gulf; the likelihood is that the bombing, apparently a culmination of local events, was in fact a response, a negative response, to international political developments, specifically to the appeals in late July 1964 by de Gaulle, U Thant, and the Soviet Union for a reconvened Geneva Conference. Despite evidence of NLF interest in these appeals for negotiations, they were rejected out-of-hand in Saigon, where the Khanh regime, increasingly impotent and *desperate for survival, publicly demanded only a short time before the bombing a show of American force against the North. In retrospect, it is possible to see in the larger context of events a version of the now familiar pattern: military and political impasse in Saigon combined with a "threat" of negotiations for political settlement producing a U.S. move to expand the war.*

The American air attack on August 5, 1964, on North Vietnam was mounted at a time when there were strong international pressures for negotiations. On July 23, 1964, the French government renewed its initiatives in the quest for a negotiated settlement of the Vietnamese conflict. At a news conference held on that day, President de Gaulle, repeating his criticisms of United States policy in Vietnam, called for a meeting "of the same order and including, in principle, the same participants as the former Geneva Conference. . . , unless Asia first, and without doubt, at a later date, the entire world, are to be plunged into very serious trials."[1] Two days later, on July 25, the Saigon government responded to the French proposal and to a similar proposal that had been issued a few days earlier by Secretary-General U Thant by stating, "The Republic of Vietnam categorically rejects the proposition directed toward the convening of a new Geneva conference, and is strongly resolved to pursue its struggle against the invaders, in spite of colonialist (i.e., French) and communist maneuvers" (*Le Monde*, July 26-27, 1964). While Khanh was angrily denouncing peace initiatives, Nguyen Huu Tho, leader of the NLF, expressed views which favored negotiations. Avoiding mention of preconditions and indicating a strong NLF interest in a compromise position, Tho stated that the NLF was prepared "to enter into negotiations with all parties, groups, sects, and patriotic individuals, without regard to differences of political points of view or past actions. . . ." "The NLF," he added, "is not opposed to the convening of an international conference in order to facilitate the search for a solution." Pointedly, he voiced his approval of Prince Sihanouk's re-

[1] Raskin, Marcus G., and Fall, Bernard B., eds., *The Vietnam Reader* (New York, 1965), p. 270.

cent suggestion for the formation of a neutral zone to encompass Laos, Cambodia, and South Vietnam (*LM*, July 26, 1964).

On the same day that the Khanh regime was fiercely rejecting the appeals of de Gaulle and U Thant, the Soviet Union made a dramatic overture. On July 25, the Soviet government urgently communicated with the fourteen nations that had participated in the Geneva Conference on Laos (1961-62) to insist that the conference be reconvened in the near future (*LM*, July 28, 1964). The Soviet initiative, intended perhaps to coincide with the efforts of U Thant and de Gaulle, was in all probability directed toward negotiated settlement in Vietnam rather than just the Laotian situation. The swift response of Hanoi to the Soviet proposal would seem to confirm this view. The North Vietnamese not only endorsed the proposal but appealed for a reconvening of the conference "as rapidly as possible . . . to preserve the independence, peace, and neutrality of Laos *and to preserve the peace of Indo-China and Southeast Asia*" (FBIS *Daily Report,* August 4, 1964; emphasis added). By August 4, the date of Hanoi's endorsement of the Soviet proposal, Peking had also announced its approval of a reconvened conference. Thus, within a two-week period, proposals for a Geneva-type conference on Vietnam and, more largely, Southeast Asia had emanated from three important sources. —U Thant, France, and the U.S.S.R.—and had been favorably received in Hanoi and Peking. None of these proposals, it should be noted, specified conditions or "preconditions" in urging that a solution be sought for the Indo-Chinese crises.

The urgency of these appeals was no more heeded in Washington than it was in Saigon. On the contrary, on July 24, the day after de Gaulle's proposal was announced, President Johnson told reporters, "We do not believe in conferences called to ratify terror, so our policy is unchanged" (*NYT*, July 25, 1964; *LM*, July 26-27, 1964). Nor was Washington any more receptive to the Soviet proposal. A commentator in *Le Monde*, referring to the Soviet message, accurately predicted the outcome: "The Soviet demand has little chance of being welcomed in Washington, where it is feared that such a conference would wish to raise the question of Vietnam" (*LM*, July 28, 1964). It may safely be assumed, in the light of President Johnson's remark, that the United States government supported the violent rejection of moves toward negotiations contained in the Saigon government's statement of July 25. Having refused "to ratify terror," the Administration, on the following day, ordered the dispatch of 5,000 to 6,000 additional U.S. troops to Vietnam, assuring the world, at the same time, that the United States had no intention of extending the war.[2]

The decision to commit more American troops to the war zone came, significantly enough, at a time when South Vietnamese officials, despite the obvious weakness of their position, began to display a new belligerency. By the summer of 1964, the recently installed government of South Vietnamese Premier Nguyen Khanh was still far from having consolidated and stabilized its political position; as yet it had not acquired either prestige or effective power. Neither dramatic victories nor even successful actions against the Vietcong had been achieved when, late in July, Premier Khanh began to call for *bac-tien,* a "march to the North," by South Vietnamese troops (*LM*, July 29, 1964). It is difficult to say whether this call for an invasion of the North was intended to be taken seriously or was merely "tough talk," for the purpose of increasing the Premier's prestige. If seriously intended, it undoubtedly implied the need for extensive American military support, for without such support an invasion of the North was inconceivable. Actually, the point is moot, for *bac-tien* did not materialize, nor did Khanh survive politically to direct it. Nevertheless, the Premier's appeal for a "march to the North" obtained a certain degree of credibility when the commander of the South Vietnamese Air Force (the now famous General Ky) revealed, at about the same time, that South Vietnamese commandos had been parachuted north of the seventeenth parallel to conduct sabotage raids (Ibid.). This was the first public acknowledgment of the raids, though, according to *Le Monde* correspondent Georges Chaffard, American-trained South Vietnamese commandos had been operating sporadically in the Tonkin area since 1957 and more intensively since 1961. Their area of operations included the region that was shortly to be projected into the news as the scene of the "Tonkin Gulf incident," and though, as Chaffard reports, their penetrations were mainly by parachute, their approach was some-

[2] The order was issued on July 25, the day following the President's news conference; it was reported by Reuters on July 27 and by *The New York Times* on July 28. See also *Le Monde,* July 28 and July 29.

times by sea (*LM*, August 7, 1964). Since operations of this kind require substantial air and sea transportation and protection, U.S. logistical and tactical support was almost certain to have been involved. To this extent, then, the new militant attitude in Saigon was committed to action against the North, or at least to a report of actions already underway, actions that presumably involved American tactical support.

The unusual bellicosity in Saigon, doubtless framed to counter the "threat" of peace moves contained in the recent international proposals, and the supporting role of Washington, both in rejecting the proposals and in committing more troops to Vietnam, may have had as their objective nothing more than a strengthening of the position of the increasingly anxious General Khanh, against whom, as persistent rumor had it, plots were being hatched. The events of the following days, however, suggest that, with a ready-made situation in hand in Tonkin Gulf, the Johnson administration had a commitment to its own policies that was more far-reaching than the one it had made to the faltering regime in Saigon.

On August 2, 1964, according to what later became the official United States version of the incident, three North Vietnamese patrol boats engaged in an unprovoked attack on American warships in the Tonkin Gulf, initiating thereby the first of the episodes that constitute "the Tonkin Gulf incident." Before August 2, however, several incidents had occurred in the same area that attest to the American "presence" there. Hanoi, on several occasions, had issued charges against the U.S. for violation of the Geneva Accords. On July 25, Radio Hanoi charged that the Americans and their "lackeys" had fired on North Vietnamese fishing vessels, which charge was included in a formal protest to the International Control Commission on the 27th. On July 30, the North Vietnamese claimed, patrol boats of the South Vietnamese naval forces again raided Northern fishing vessels in Tonkin Gulf and subsequently, under the protective cover of the U.S. destroyer *Maddox,* bombarded the islands of Hon Me and Hon Ngu. The bombardment of these islands was the subject of a protest to the I.C.C. on July 31, announcement of which was broadcast by Radio Hanoi on August 1.[3] The action in the area on August 2 was evidently

[3] *Le Monde,* August 4, 1964. Refusing to comment on the charges, Secretary McNamara stated at the time the United States

not an isolated incident. According to the North Vietnamese version of the encounter on August 2, an American ship had penetrated North Vietnamese territorial waters the previous evening and was subsequently engaged by three North Vietnamese torpedo boats.[4] It was later confirmed that U.S. planes, which quickly arrived on the scene, sank one of the torpedo boats and seriously damaged the other two. The American warship, the destroyer *Maddox,* suffered no damage in the encounter.[5]

If it is true that American ships had been lending support to South Vietnamese commandos in the Tonkin area, then the Hanoi version, accusing the *Maddox* of having violated the territorial waters of North Vietnam in this area, seems plausible. But even if the American version of an "unprovoked" attack is taken as factual, it is difficult to look upon this incident as a major provocation on the part of the North Vietnamese. That small torpedo boats would risk an engagement with an American destroyer in international waters seems less than likely, but even if such a foolhardy expedition had been mounted, the result was inevitably a minor naval victory for the United States, and the case presented no real issue of provocation. Indeed, Washington announced on the following day that it did not consider the incident to have been a "major crisis" (*LM,* August 4-5, 1964), and a Pentagon spokesman remarked that the situation was "unwelcome, but not especially serious." [6] The one significant response in Washington was President Johnson's directive to the military regarding enemy attacks: where previously standing orders to U.S. warships were to *repel* enemy attackers, they now read *destroy* (*LM,* August 5, 1964).

While Washington was apparently responding with prudence and forbearance to the incident of August 2, in Saigon Premier Khanh, still bellicose, and trusting perhaps that an

---

was not in communication with the South Vietnamese government on such matters (*Le Monde,* August 9 and 10, 1964).

[4] Like many nations, North Vietnam recognizes a 12-mile territorial limit rather than a 3-mile limit, accepted by the United States. It has been conceded officially that the *USS Maddox* "went in at least 11 miles in order to show that we do not recognize a 12-mile limit" (*The Viet-nam Reader,* p. 311; *Congressional Record,* August 6, 1964, p. 18407).

[5] A full account appears in *Le Monde,* August 5-8, 1964.

[6] *The New York Times,* August 3, 1964. The State Department announced the following day a decision to make an official protest.

American show of force would strengthen his hand, seized the opportunity to fan the flames. "The Americans," he declaimed publicly, "should seize this occasion to dissipate the enemy's belief according to which the United States is only a paper tiger" (*LM*, August 5, 1964).

Almost immediately another "occasion" presented itself, and obligingly the "tiger" lunged. On August 5, in retaliation for an alleged attack the previous day on the U.S. destroyers *Maddox* and *Turner Joy* by an undetermined number of North Vietnamese PT boats, in which, it was said, two of the latter were sunk, the United States mounted heavy air attacks on three major North Vietnam coastal bases; the bases were demolished, twenty-five boats were destroyed or damaged, and, according to Secretary McNamara, the local fuel depots were almost totally destroyed (*NYT*, August 6, 1964; *LM*, August 6, 1964). President Johnson reported to the American people on the "occasion" that prompted the retaliatory air strikes. North Vietnamese officials denied that any naval encounter had occurred on August 4, as the Americans had claimed, and were vehement in protesting that the entire incident was an American "fabrication." Alain Clement, Washington correspondent for *Le Monde*, wrily commented, ". . . the record of the American retaliation . . . is more complete than that of the naval aggression that was supposedly the cause. . . ." (*LM*, August 8, 1964). The United States, it has been pointed out, failed to present any photographic evidence of the August 4 incident, as has commonly been done in American presentations to the United Nations Security Council. But even if, once again, the American account is accepted as factual, the incident appears to be nothing more than a casual naval skirmish in which the United States, having suffered no damage to its vessels, again emerged as the victor; retaliation would seem to have consisted in the routing of the enemy.

It is difficult, therefore, to believe that the naval clash of August 4 (if such there was) provided the actual motive for so drastic a move as the bombing of North Vietnam on August 5. One immediate result of the bombing was noted on the following day by a Reuters correspondent in Saigon, who reported that the position of General Khanh now "appears to have been consolidated," observers there agreeing that the evolution of events had reinforced the political status of the Premier. Evidently Khanh was now able to demonstrate to his political opponents that he was not tied to a "paper tiger" but to an ally that was willing to expand the war to support his cause.

At his press conference on July 24, less than two weeks before the bombing, President Johnson had warned, "It is true that there is danger and provocation from the North, and such provocation could cause a response," but he nevertheless affirmed his intention not to extend the war (*NYT*, July 25, 1964). An opportunity for a response to "provocation" came—or, as Hanoi would have it, had been "fabricated"—and the action was swift and drastic.

While there were, at this juncture, no further American attacks on North Vietnam, the nature of the United States "commitment" was patently altered; as later events indicate, the bombing set a precedent and marked a new stage of active intervention in the conflict. Not without significance also is the fact that at the very moment when the "Tonkin Gulf incident" was breeding American escalation, the North Vietnamese were making overtures, by way of Secretary-General U Thant, for meetings with U.S. representatives in Rangoon. These overtures, which the U.S. ignored for some months and then rejected, were not made public until the following year (Bernard Fall, *NYT*, December 12, 1965). The thunderous voice of American power stilled both international and local voices that were appealing for negotiation, at least for the duration of the presidential campaign in the United States; General Khanh's hand in the uncertain situation in Saigon had been strengthened, his position was apparently consolidated, and his government could be expected to last at least through the November elections in the U.S.[7]

While no conclusive interpretation of the events of late July and early August 1964 can be arrived at on the basis of the available evidence, a reasonable summary of causes and effects relevant to American involvement in Vietnam is possi-

[7] Despite the dramatic show of American power, in part at least on Khanh's behalf, the inherent weakness of the "strongman" was soon demonstrated. Apparently believing that his own position had been strengthened, on August 7 Khanh proclaimed a state of emergency in Saigon, outlawed all strikes and demonstrations, intensified the censorship, and stepped up police intimidation of the civilian population. Khanh's openly stated aims in instituting these measures was to "eliminate the Communists and their *neutralist* (italics ours) sympathizers" (*Le Monde*, August 8, 9, 1965). Finally, on August 17, General Nguyen Khanh proclaimed himself chief of state and of government, that is, the supreme leader

ble. At a time when the political situation in Saigon was again deteriorating, and thereby threatening the alleged legitimacy of the American "presence," Premier Khanh began to call for aggressive action against North Vietnam to reinforce his shaky personal position. At a time when international pressures for bringing the problems of Indo-China to the conference table were intensified, the United States not only openly revealed its disinclination to participate but mounted a large-scale bombardment subsequent to an incident, on August 2, which U.S. officials termed minor and to a second incident, on August 4, which, if it actually occurred, terminated in an American victory. Thus, the bombardment of North Vietnam was not only out of all proportion to the incidents alleged to have caused it; it served to worsen a climate which was becoming increasingly favorable to a negotiated settlement and concomitantly, in behalf of larger American objectives, it served to prop up the tottering regime of Premier Nguyen Khanh.

---

of South Vietnam. However, barely two days had elapsed before the resilience of the opposition was again revealed. Beginning with criticism by two prominent Buddhist leaders and culminating in demonstrations by many thousands of Buddhists and students in Saigon, Hué, and Danang, the opposition mounted its cause, and General Khanh, apparently under American pressure, was forced to relinquish his position on August 25. Although his retreat was only partial (the Khanh dictatorship was replaced by a triumvirate of which Khanh was a member), the showdown indicated that Buddhist opposition would continue to be a powerful factor to be reckoned with. (See *Le Monde,* August 18 through August 26.)

IV

The Kosygin Visit and the Bombing of North Vietnam (January—February 1965)

SUMMARY: The key date of this period is February 7, 1965, when the United States began a bombing of North Vietnam that has remained virtually continuous down to the present. The United States decided to bomb after a period of unprecedented antigovernment and anti-American demonstrations in the cities of South Vietnam, and only a little more than a week after a new coup brought a junta to power whose commitment to continue the war appeared increasingly dubious. Moreover, both before and after February 7, various international moves were afoot to arrange a negotiated settlement of the war. Disintegration in Saigon and the gathering strength of these diplomatic moves had led a number of foreign journalists to predict that the war would be over in six months. The events of February 7 in themselves halted neither the agitation in Saigon nor the international diplomatic moves. However, in the course of February, the hard-liners in the Saigon government strengthened their position, notably through the final ouster of General Nguyen Khanh, and the United States moved once and for all to continuing and systematic bombing of North Vietnamese military targets.

We have already seen how, in January 1964, domestic unrest and pressures to end the war were cut off by a military coup, of which local U.S. authorities were at the very least not unaware. In January 1965, there was a renewed outbreak of proneutralist, antigovernment, and increasingly anti-American demonstrations; a general strike in Hué on January 7

(LM, January 8, 1965) spread within a week to Danang, where employees at the U.S. air base failed to turn up for work (LM, January 13). At least two Saigon papers published editorials deploring the continuation of the war and demanding negotiations (LM, January 7, 1965.) Leaflets in Hué and Danang attacked the Huong regime of the moment as servile collaborators with the Americans (LM, January 15, 1965). On January 17, police fired on demonstrators in Hué and Dalat, wounding four students (NYT, January 18, 1965, p. 1). A few days later, thirty were wounded as police and paratroopers dispersed a Buddhist demonstration of 5,000 in Saigon (LM, January 21, 1965). On January 22, 500 Buddhists demonstrated in front of the U.S. Embassy, and the USIS library at Hué was sacked (LM, January 23, 1965). In the wake of these disturbances, the civilian Huong regime was finally overthrown on January 27 by a military group headed by Nguyen Khanh (NYT, January 27, 1965, p. 1). But unrest persisted within the country, together with evidence of deep divisions within this junta and repeated rumors of a possible negotiated settlement (NYT, January 29, 1965, p. 1; February 3, p. 1; February 5, p. 2). The crisis, however, was primarily domestic rather than military; in fact on February 3, the United States Military Assistance Command in Saigon described the month of January 1965 "as the most successful month of Government military operations to date" (NYT, February 4, 1965, p. 3).

This state of extreme internal confusion was to some extent stabilized after the decision of the United States to bomb North Vietnam, on February 7. At the time, we were told that this was in response to a guerilla raid on Pleiku in which eight Americans were killed; but we now know that no more than twelve hours elapsed between the beginning of the Pleiku raid and the dropping of bombs on North Vietnam.

Meanwhile McGeorge Bundy (who had flown to Saigon shortly before the raid) said on his return *that the immediate effect of the Pleiku and North Vietnamese raids was to pull together American and Vietnamese leaders (NYT, February 9, 1965, p. 12). Under the circumstances, this significant United States escalation could not but have the effect of demonstrating to all South Vietnamese, government and opposition alike, the determination of the United States to continue the war.*[1]

Premier Kosygin was in Hanoi at the time of the U.S. escalation; it has been alleged that he came with proposals for mediating the conflict.[2] *On February 23, the Russians and French began high-level consultations in Paris concerning such a possibility; and de Gaulle called publicly for negotiations without preconditions.*[3] *On February 24, U Thant made a similar appeal, saying that "the great American people, if only they know the true facts and the background to the developments in South Vietnam, will agree with me that further bloodshed is unnecessary" (NYT, February 25, 1965, p. 1). On February 26, Premier Kosygin for the first time alluded publicly to*

[1] Senator Everett Dirksen blandly commented, "If we hadn't given an adequate response, we might have given the impression we might pull out" (*NYT*, February 9, 1965, p. 13).

[2] This was the expectation in Washington at the time of Bundy's departure for Saigon. *The New York Times* spoke of "the developing speculation in the Administration . . . that Mr. Kosygin's trip might be the opening move in a broad Soviet attempt to mediate between the United States and the Hanoi regime for a settlement of the Vietnamese war" (*NYT*, February 2, 1965, p. 2).

[3] The surprising role of the Soviet Union in this period was depicted clearly by the Chinese in November: "Johnson wanted to play his fraudulent game of 'unconditional discussions.' So the new leaders of the CPSU put forward the idea of 'unconditional negotiations.' On February 16 this year, the day after Kosygin's return to Moscow, the Soviet government officially put before Vietnam and China a proposal to convene a new international conference on Indo-China without prior conditions, which in fact was advocacy of 'unconditional negotiations' on the Vietnam question. On February 23, disregarding the stand which the Vietnamese government had taken against this proposal and without waiting for a reply from China, the new leaders of the CPSU discussed the question of calling the above-mentioned international conference with the President of France through the Soviet ambassador" (Peking *People's Daily*, November 11, 1965).

the possibility of finding "at a conference table the measures permitting a solution of Indo-Chinese problems" (LM, March 3, 1965; see below. Previously the Russians had talked only of a Conference on Laos or Cambodia). Meanwhile, on February 24, the U.S. Air Force announced publicly that it was using its own jets in air strikes against the NLF, thus abandoning any pretense to an advisory role. The New York Times, reporting this announcement, commented: "The acknowledgment of the change had the effect of stiffening Washington's position in the face of continuing appeals abroad for negotiations" (NYT, February 25, 1965, p. 1). On February 27, with great fanfare, the State Department released its White Paper, which endeavored to prove that the war was not "a local rebellion": "In Vietnam a Communist government has set out deliberately to conquer a sovereign people in a neighboring state." [4]

As 1964 came to an end, both the military and the political situation in South Vietnam began to deteriorate rapidly. The Vietcong were able to mount larger operations, such as the battle of Binh Ghia, early in January 1965.[5] Reports

[4] Facts were necessary to support this claim, and a certain "escalation" can be observed in U. S. estimates of infiltration from North Vietnam during this period. On July 29, 1964, a U. S. military spokesman suggested at a news conference "that roughly 10,000 men had infiltrated from the North over the last five years" (*NYT*, January 27, 1965, p. 2). On January 26, 1965, it was reported from Saigon that "United States intelligence agencies have sharply increased their estimate" to "at least 19,300 men . . . for a period only seven months longer" (Ibid.). To this figure was then added a further 15,000 "based on information from only one source" (Ibid.). As for the net importance of all this, "United States officials here have attributed to this aid a weight no greater than 20 percent in explaining the headway being made by the Vietcong" (Ibid.). The White Paper itself estimates infiltration of "nearly 20,000" and "probably 17,000 more infiltrators" (*NYT*, February 28, 1965, p. 30).

[5] How much of this increased effort was due to infiltration from the North remains a murky question, one which the State Department White Paper did not answer satisfactorily. Jean Lacouture, *Le Monde* correspondent, wrote in May 1965 that until the middle of 1964 only ten percent of the Vietcong's weapons came from the North; in the last six months of 1964,

from Saigon reflected an increasing pessimism within American military circles. More significant, however, for the events of February 1965 were the political changes in the Saigon government.

Despite Premier Khanh's consolidation of power in August 1964, political instability had continued to plague the Saigon government. On September 13, General Lam Van Phat attempted a coup against Khanh. A tribal revolt broke out late the same month. However, with the appointment of a civilian, Tran Van Huong, as premier on November 1, some semblance of stability appeared to have returned. On December 4, South Vietnam's military leaders announced support for the Huong government. The United States and specifically Ambassador Maxwell Taylor voiced their full support for the Huong government. Yet on December 20, a new coup erupted which deposed Premier Huong. American reaction was immediate and hostile. Ambassador Taylor exerted strong pressure on the "young Turks" to restore civilian government, and early in January, Premier Huong was returned to his position.

As every observer has written, South Vietnamese politics are complicated. However, from the few analyses available, we shall try to sketch out a general picture to explain the December events. In an article published in April 1965, two special correspondents of the *New York Herald Tribune*, Pham Xuan An and Beverly Deepe, identified three camps: (1) a "pro-Neutralist and pro-Buddhist wing," led by General Nguyen Chanh Thi; (2) a "rigid anti-Communist hard-line wing," led by General Nguyen Van Thieu; and (3) the "pro-French moderates," led by General Duong Van Minh (*NYHT*, April 11, 1965). Robert Shaplen, the well-informed *New Yorker* correspondent, has made a similar analysis, with stress on the first two groups. An, Deepe, and Shaplen agree that General Thi has close connections with the Buddhist monk Tri Quang, whose views An and Deepe describe as "anti-Catholic, anti-American, and pro-Neutralist." General Thieu is also, by general agreement, regarded as the leader of the militant anti-Communist, generally Catholic, right wing.

With these three camps in mind, let us look at the coup of December 20, 1964. Prior to then, the Duong Van Minh group, the "pro-French moderates," appears to have lost

---

the percentage rose to twenty-five percent (*New Republic*, May 22, 1965). Cf. *I.F. Stone's Weekly*, March 8, 1965, on the White Paper.

power; Minh himself lost his place on October 26 as titular "chief of state," a post to which Khanh had reluctantly appointed him. Just prior to December 20, the Huong government announced the retirement of large numbers of military men, many of whom appeared to be associated with Duong Van Minh. Thus the elimination of the third group produced a growing polarization between the Thi and Thieu factions, a process apparently receiving the support of the American government. Buddhist demonstrations began to erupt at about this time, adding to a growing pressure against the government. The leader of the December 20 coup was General Nguyen Chanh Thi, seconded by Air Vice-Marshal Nguyen Cao Ky. Ky's position has never been very clear, but available analyses show him to have been in association with Thi, though apparently not completely committed to his views. Khanh himself was not directly involved in the December 20 coup, but came to its support almost immediately.[6]

The political scene was dominated by Buddhist-led strikes and demonstrations. On January 3, with the Saigon government again on the verge of collapse, thousands of South Vietnamese demonstrated in Saigon. Despite government warnings that in the future demonstrators would be dispersed by force, more demonstrations took place in Saigon the next day. At Hué, demonstrating Buddhists and students appealed for a two-day general strike. Faced with general contempt for its authority, the Saigon government confessed, "The authority of the government is trampled under—martial law is not being respected—the forces of law and order have lost control." On the seventh, Hué was almost completely paralyzed by a general strike called by protesters against the regime; in Saigon two newspapers, *Viet Nam Nouveau* and *Journal d'Extreme Orient*, published editorials that deplored continuation of the war and demanded negotiations (*LM*, January 8, 1965). By January 13, the protest strikes had spread to Danang, and Vietnamese employees of the Ameri-

[6] Khanh issued an order of the day with a strong anti-American tone (*LM*, Dec. 24, 1964). Ambassador Taylor reportedly reacted by saying that henceforth the Americans would be "one hundred percent opposed" to Khanh. The growing feud between Khanh and Taylor was widely reported at the time; it was generally recognized that one or the other had to go. Taylor put great pressure on Huong to stand firm (*LM*, Dec. 27-28, 1964).

can air base there failed to report for work (*LM,* January 13, 1965).

By January 10, the contending government factions had agreed to a compromise, and an uneasy calm prevailed in Saigon. However, Buddhist attacks against the Huong government and against Ambassador Taylor increased in intensity. From the statements of the demonstrators and their Buddhist leaders, it is clear that they regarded Tran Van Huong as an American puppet and wanted him entirely out of the government. The Saigon government responded with a truculent announcement: "The anti-Communist and anti-neutralist position of the generals of the forces of the Republic of Vietnam remains clear and resolute" (*LM,* January 13, 1965). This statement immediately became the target of the demonstrators. Leaflets distributed in Hué and Danang said the announcement was imposed by the Americans "in order to permit them to continue the struggle which they are conducting against the Communists in Vietnam;" the Americans are anxious to keep Huong in power, the leaflets charged, because "they cannot find more servile collaborators." The appeal of one handbill epitomized the entire protest movement: "The Vietnam population reclaims their right to democratic self-determination" (*LM,* January 14, 1965). The mounting pressure of the demonstrations provoked the junta to action. On January 19, police fired on anti-government demonstrators in Dalat, killing at least three. The same day, Saigon announced a reshuffling of generals in the Huong cabinet. Huong seems to have made a conciliatory gesture to the military (*LM,* January 19, 1965), inviting not "soft-line" Thi but "hard-line" Thieu into the government. The Buddhists at once reaffirmed their total opposition to the government, accusing it of "profiting from support of the Americans and former Diemists" in applying a policy aimed at division and destruction of Buddhism (*LM,* January 21, 1965). On January 22, police and paratroopers put down a demonstration of 5,000 Buddhists in Saigon, wounding at least 30. (*LM,* January 22, 1965). The next day, 500 demonstrated before the American Embassy and broke windows of the U.S. Information Service library. At this point, preparations long underway for election of a National Congress were abandoned (*LM,* January 26, 1965).

On January 27, another coup, led by Nguyen Khanh and Nguyen Chanh Thi, deposed the civilian government and returned Khanh to power. The American view, reported from

Saigon, was that a Buddhist-military coalition government would now arise which would negotiate with the National Liberation Front (*LM*, January 28, 1965).[7] Catholic opposition was made immediately apparent, and directed squarely against Khanh. Joseph Alsop, on January 31, wrote ominously of an impending defeat in South Vietnam which could lead to the crumbling of the American position in Thailand and the Philippines. He attributed Sihanouk's anti-American policy in Laos to his expectation of American defeat in South Vietnam, and even postulated it as a major factor in de Gaulle's policies.

The time was ripe, as it was not to be again, for decorous American disengagement. Vocal elements of a war-weary people were pleading for peace, advocating negotiations, and demanding expulsion of the "foreigners." The morale of the South Vietnamese military forces had sagged to a new low, as the desertion rate—30 percent in January 1965—revealed. And the government of the "Republic of Vietnam" had become a mockery, by its own admission held in contempt by the people and powerless to act effectively. The manifestation of overwhelming American power during the Tonkin Gulf "incident" had won little friendship for the United States among Vietnamese of the South, either from admiration or fear. The American "presence," except to a few in power, was patently unwanted. Clearly, a decision by the United States government to remain and prosecute the war against the rebels and the North could scarcely be justified as a defense of the freedom of the South Vietnamese—who had vociferously demonstrated their desire to be free of American intervention. Such a decision would be, inevitably, a commitment to transform a local civil war into an American adventure, with the prize supremacy in Asia.

Reports of the rioting in South Vietnam, of the increasingly deteriorating military situation, and of the appalling impotence of the Saigon regimes provoked contradictory, but predictable, responses in Washington. Senators Morse, Mansfield, Monroney and Cooper publicly expressed serious doubts about the wisdom and the relevance of American policy. Senator Russell, later to be identified as a fierce advocate of expanded hostilities, seized the initiative and called for Senate

[7] Jean Lacouture wrote in *Le Monde* that Nguyen Khanh might be undergoing a *reconversion*, envisaging himself now as the leader of a government which would negotiate peace for his country.

debate on Vietnam policy (*LM*, January 12, 1965). The position of the Administration, less and less clear on the surface, was evidently already converging toward that of General Maxwell Taylor, who reportedly maintained, "We ought to carry on and never give up because we are frustrated and discouraged" (*LM*, January 11, 1965).[8] By late January it began to appear that the Administration's new policy in regard to the Vietnam conflict was fully formulated. Administration spokesman McGeorge Bundy, once of the opinion that the Vietnamese should be left to go it alone, expressed strong doubts about the capacity of the South Vietnamese to cope with the Vietcong unaided; extension of the war, he said, depended upon the degree of infiltration from North Vietnam (*NYT*, January 24, 1965; *LM*, January 25, 1965).[9]

It will be recalled that in the months following the fall of Ngo Dinh Diem in November 1963, and also in July and August of 1964, various initiatives had been taken to seek a negotiated solution (see above). This was also the case early in 1965. An important sign that the climate for negotiations was improving was the increasingly important role of the U.S.S.R., as opposed to China, in Hanoi. Supporters of Administration policy have often argued that the pro-Soviet wing in Hanoi was "moderate" and would be willing to negotiate. Jean Lacouture, the *Le Monde* correspondent, has

[8] On January 27, Ambassador Taylor went to Vientiane and Bangkok. We cannot be sure of the reasons for his absence, but it most likely was bound up with intensified American air activity in Laos. On December 29, General Phoumi Nosavan, head of the right wing forces in Laos, visited Saigon. Shortly thereafter, the United States began openly to bomb Pathet Lao targets in Laos. On February 4, Premier Souvana Phouma denounced Phoumi. As American air activity in Laos intensified, there were increasing reports of attacks against North Vietnamese villages. Thus, on January 5, Hanoi accused the Americans and the South Vietnamese of launching such attacks (*LM*, January 5, 1965). On January 23, the United States State Department accused North Vietnam of wanting to provoke a clash with the United States.

[9] Speculation on American choices had been heard frequently during January. On January 9, the London *Economist* reported that the situation was deteriorating in South Vietnam, and that "to put it right it will almost certainly be necessary to mount air strikes against North Vietnamese targets" (p. 94). Western correspondents in Saigon were reported as predicting, even after the coup, "the emergence within six months of a government that will present an ultimatum-invitation to the United States to get out of South Vietnam" (London *Economist*, January 30, 1965, p. 419).

reported the continuing prevalence of pro-Soviet attitudes among the highest echelons of North Vietnamese leadership (*Vietnam: Between Two Truces,* p. 230). The announcement of Premier Kosygin's visit to Hanoi in early February indicated that Soviet influence was again on the rise in Hanoi; and American observers saw in his visit signs that Moscow and Hanoi were both thinking of negotiations:

> Now again the Asian Communists, this time in South Vietnam, seem ready to bid for power through a negotiated settlement. The Soviet Union, apparently fearful that a continuation of the war in South Vietnam *may lead to United States bombing of North Vietnam and its own involvement,* is reappearing in the role of a diplomatic agent (*NYT*, February 5, 1965, p. 2; emphasis added).[10]

Moreover, there were signs that the NLF was moving in a pro-Soviet direction. On January 1, 1965, Moscow announced that the NLF had reached agreement with the Soviet government to set up a permanent delegation in Moscow (*LM,* January 1, 1965). The Soviet move was evidently designed to counter the influence of Peking, which had welcomed the establishment of an NLF delegation in September, following the Tonkin Gulf affair. Although the evidence is fragmentary, this and other instances suggest that when the war situation becomes more grave, both North Vietnam and the NLF tend to move in the direction of Peking, and, conversely, when prospects for a peaceful solution appear, they favor the stance of the U.S.S.R.

Early in January, Foreign Minister Gromyko pledged North Vietnam Soviet aid in the event of attack (*LM*, January 5, 1965). New trade agreements were signed between the Soviet Union and North Vietnam. These Soviet moves must be seen, however, in the light of continuing friendly gestures by the Soviets toward the United States. On January 8, *Izvestia* called for a meeting between President Johnson and Premier Kosygin. On February 5, President Johnson reciprocated and said he would like to visit the U.S.S.R.

[10] Thus the record seems to challenge President Johnson's claim to Congress on May 4, 1965, that "when we began the bombings (i.e. of North Vietnam on February 7) there was no talk of negotiations" (Dept. of State *Bulletin,* May 24, 1965, p. 818).

What was in the wind may be seen in the remarks of a *Le Monde* correspondent, who wrote, "the Russians generally admit that one must help the United States save face in this sector," [11] namely Vietnam (*LM*, February 5, 1965). The purpose of Soviet diplomatic moves was not lost on the Chinese; on January 19, Peking accused the Soviet leaders of practicing Khrushchevism without Khrushchev (*LM*, January 19, 1965).

The *rapprochement* between Moscow and Hanoi culminated in the Kosygin visit. On February 3, the North Vietnamese press published lavish praise of the Soviet Union. Kosygin arrived on February 6. Early in the morning of Sunday, February 7 (Vietnam time), a small band of Vietcong attacked the American base at Pleiku. About twelve hours later American planes started attacking North Vietnam in force.

On February 8, while the high-level Soviet delegation conferred with officials in Hanoi, U.S. planes began to bomb North Vietnam. This extraordinary tactic was said to be a response to a Vietcong attack on the American base at Pleiku.

The time of the Pleiku incident was Saturday afternoon in Washington. Clearly, American planes must already have been poised for the attack, since no more than twelve hours elapsed between the *beginning* of the mortar shelling at Pleiku and the first dropping of bombs. One is forced to conclude that the attack had been planned in advance, and that a sudden decision was made that Pleiku constituted a suitable pretext.

The attack on North Vietnam, at a time when the Soviet premier was there, was clearly a challenge to the Soviets, who only a short time before had promised their aid to North Vietnam in case of attack.[12] Kosygin concluded his visit to

[11] That the Russians actually had such intentions was confirmed in a bitter letter addressed by the Chinese Communists to the Soviet Central Committee on November 11, 1965, where the Chinese accused the Russians of having tried to help the United States find an honorable solution to the Vietnamese dilemma.

[12] It might be noted that several times after February 7, newspapers reported comments of American officials that the raids against the North had not been followed by any concrete response from the Communist side. Apparently one of the dialogues current in Washington for some time had been whether U. S. military action against North Vietnam would or would not bring about active intervention by China, Russia, or both. W. W. Rostow was reported by *Newsweek* (March 9, 1964) to have argued, in advocating his plan No. 6 for escalating attacks on North Viet-

Hanoi and returned to Moscow after a brief stop in Peking, where he conferred with Mao Tse-tung. We know from the Chinese letter of November 11 that Mao had proposed joint action against the United States, whereas Kosygin still insisted on finding some peaceful solution to the conflict.

Despite an initial public hardening of the Soviet attitude, Kosygin resumed his efforts to promote an international conference on Indo-China. On February 16, one day after his return to Moscow, Russia submitted to Peking and Hanoi a formal proposal to call a new international conference on Indo-China (Bernard Fall, *NYT* Magazine, December 12, 1965). On February 23, Kosygin approached the French government about this proposal. Two days after the bombing, on February 10, President de Gaulle had issued a call for reconvening a Geneva Conference to discuss the future of Southeast Asia (*NYT*, February 23, 1965). The French let it be known that North Vietnam had urged France to intensify efforts for a negotiated settlement, and that the Chinese would be prepared to attend such a conference. In this proposal, withdrawal of American forces was not to be a precondition, but an eventual result of negotiations.

The response of Washington officials to de Gaulle's appeal was short and sharp: France had been given no "mandate" to act as mediator; the United States was not interested in a return to the conference table at this time (*NYT*, February 23, 1965). The Administration's refusal to consider negotiations was underscored by Secretary McNamara's reiteration of the American commitment to South Vietnam on February 19 and by the publication of the State Department White Paper late in the same month.

In spite of increasing American intransigence on the issue of negotiated settlement, powerful forces on the international scene continued to press for accommodation. On February 23, the U.S.S.R., still risking the antagonism of certain nations in the Communist sphere, added its voice to that of France in calling again for a reconvening of the Geneva Conference to negotiate a peaceful settlement of the conflict (Drew Middleton, *NYT*, February 25, 1965). On the same day, Secretary-General U Thant, at an extraordinary press conference, revealed that he had been conducting pri-

nam, that "the situation in North Vietnam is so precarious and the Sino-Soviet split so deep that there is little danger of massive retaliation from the Communist bloc." For the continuing prevalence of this view, see James Reston, *NYT*, April 27, 1966.

vate discussions on the question of Vietnam for a long time and that he was now prepared to recommend preliminary moves designed to produce a workable conference and, hopefully, a peaceful settlement (*NYT*, February 25, 1965). France, the Soviet Union, and North Vietnam were prompt in announcing their support of the Secretary-General's recommendations (Hamilton, *NYT*, February 25, 1965). Revealing some of his evident vexation at the stiffened posture of the Johnson administration, U Thant took the occasion to remind American officials of certain truths: "The political and diplomatic method of discussions and negotiations alone," he said, "can create conditions which will enable the United States to withdraw gracefully from that part of the world." Appealing to the American public at large, he remarked, "I am sure that the great American people, if only they know the true facts and the background to the developments in South Vietnam, will agree with me that further bloodshed is unnecessary." The implications were clear when he reminded his audience that "in times of war and of hostilities the first casualty is truth" (*NYT*, February 25, 1965).

The Secretary-General, who had maintained a discreet silence throughout the preceding months of anxiety, had set a thankless task for himself, for the response of the United States government was curt: "There are no authorized negotiations underway with Mr. Thant" (Gottlieb, *Sane World*, September 1965). His plan was formally rejected (*NYT*, March 10, 1965).

While efforts to promote negotiations continued to be rejected or ignored in Washington, the situation in Saigon remained unchanged. Demonstrations continued to erupt in various cities of South Vietnam. In fact, as February drew toward a close, explicit calls for a negotiated peace were more openly heard in South Vietnam. On February 16, troops fired on a large group of demonstrators in Danang. Several leaders were arrested, and one man was sentenced to death, a move apparently supported by General Thi. On February 26, *Le Monde* again reported from Saigon rumors about impending peace talks (*LM*, February 25, 1965).[13] In sum, agitation aimed at putting pressure on the Quat government to explore avenues for negotiations was widespread and con-

[13] Cf. *NYT*, March 4, 1965, p. 10: "The prospect of a Buddhist government in South Vietnam willing to recognize Vietcong politicians is not remote, according to diplomatic observers."

tinuous. Significantly, these moves were supported by members of religious sects other than the Buddhists, notably the Hoa Hao, the Cao Dai, and some Catholics.

While popular pressures for negotiations continued throughout February, significant changes were occurring within the Saigon government. On February 19, a new coup was attempted in Saigon, led by one Colonel Phan Ngoc Thao. Thao came from one of South Vietnam's most prominent Catholic families and earlier had been attached to the South Vietnamese Embassy in Washington. He was described by the *Le Monde* correspondent as "one of the fiercest enemies" of General Nguyen Chanh Thi. The general interpretation was that the forces behind Colonel Thao were the old Diemist officers trying to make a comeback. The Thao coup was reportedly supported by Tran Thien Khiem, then ambassador to the United States (*LM*, February 20, 21, 22, 1965). Ambassador Khiem, one might note, had been closely associated with then General Nguyen Khanh in the coup of January 30, 1964. The coup leaders announced the deposition of Khanh and their intention of setting up a government of resistance against Communism and neutralism. Saigon radio, in the hands of the Thao forces, began to praise Ngo Dinh Diem and, interestingly, attacked Henry Cabot Lodge, implying that he had aided the anti-Diem forces in the overthrow of the old leader. Since the coup was started by the right-wing, a reaction from the left-wing was inevitable. The following day, General Thi, who had been in consultation with Buddhist and student leaders, succeeded in recapturing Saigon, and reestablished General Khanh, for a moment at least, in power. During those days, *The New York Times* carried dispatches from Saigon reporting that Vietcong elements had infiltrated the highest levels of the army.

What happened in the hours after Thi's recapture of power is unclear. On February 23, it was announced that General Tran Van Minh ("Little Minh") had taken over command of the armed forces. Little Minh was a moderate Catholic, and appears to have been considered a member of a pro-French middle-of-the-road group, to which his namesake Duong Van Minh also belonged. Perhaps the most significant shift in the power constellation was the decline of Thi and the elevation of Nguyen Cao Ky (*LM*, February 23, 1965). The evidence for this break is the composition of the new five-man supreme military committee, announced on March 5. The committee was headed by General Nguyen Van Thieu, and included Ky as a member, but not Thi, who remained as the commander of the first corps area, based at Danang. The events following the Thao coup did have one clear-cut result. Nguyen Khanh was eliminated and shortly thereafter was exiled from the country.

Every report from Saigon at that time reflected confusion; no one appeared to know exactly what had happened. However, in retrospect a pattern may be discerned. As we have stated, even after Khanh was eliminated, dispatches reported the continuing interest of the Quat government in finding a peaceful solution. In mid-April, Phan Huy Quat's deputy premier, Tran Van Tuyen, gave an interview to *Le Monde* in which he said: "This war must be stopped. . . . It is necessary to create a government with roots in the masses. . . . In such a context, the left-wing South Vietnamese forces could find a place. . . ." (*Viet Report,* July, 1965). As a result, Quat was bitterly attacked, particularly by Catholic elements. Thus it would appear that the civilian and essentially Buddhist elements around Quat still leaned toward a peaceful solution. However, the makeup of the five-man military committee, headed, it will be recalled, by General Thieu, was dominated by hard-line elements, newly reinforced by the adherence of Air Vice-Marshal Nguyen Cao Ky. The question as to who would win out in the end, Quat or the combined Ky-Thieu forces, was settled on June 11, when the Quat government fell and was replaced by a military junta dominated by Ky and Thieu.

The course of U.S. air escalation during February also followed an interesting pattern in its choice of targets. After the initial American attack of February 7 on North Vietnam, no further attacks were made by U.S. planes until March 2, although South Vietnamese planes staged a major air attack on North Vietnam on February 12. However, within South Vietnam and Laos, U.S. air activity intensified. On February 19, Danang-based U.S. planes attacked Communist forces in Laos. On February 24, the United States, for the first time, admitted officially that U.S. planes were directly participating in government operations against the Vietcong (*NYT,* February 25, 1965). On the following day, more U.S. jet planes were thrown into the fight against the Vietcong.

U.S. actions in Vietnam are perhaps best seen at two levels, one general and the other specific. Since President Kennedy's decision in 1961 to send major military and economic assistance to South Vietnam, the United States had pursued a policy intended to prevent a Communist victory. However, it was apparently not until the discussion in 1964 of Rostow's double-pronged plan No. 6 that Washington envisaged the bombing of North Vietnam as a means of checking both Vietcong successes and political disintegration in the South. The Tonkin Gulf incident marked the first test of that policy. Thus, one can conclude that at least since August 1964, the United States had decided on a general policy of bombing the North. However, there remains the question of the specific timing of the attacks.

As we point out in other sections of this study, a remarkably large number of U.S. attacks occurred when moves toward negotiations were afoot or when the Saigon government was in danger of falling into the hands of a faction that favored negotiations. The timing of U.S. escalation in February suggests that both factors were probably involved. The Soviet Union, France, U Thant, and possibly even North Vietnam were pressing their efforts to secure negotiations, as we have noted. In Saigon, rumors of negotiations were spreading. *Le Monde* reported on February 26 that "initiatives in favor of peace are growing in Saigon." Neutralist talk was prominent in several Saigon newspapers.

If American escalation was timed to head off peace moves, then one might ask: How was this possible? Here we enter the realm of interpretation, and we are aware of the hazards this presents to the historian who is obliged to deal with insufficient facts. The material presented so far has been based on current accounts, and our main contribution has been to present reports revealing a recurring pattern of political decay in Saigon, international peace moves, and American escalation. What we say now is our own interpretation.

We know that after the second American escalation in February, the positions of Hanoi and of the NLF stiffened, as their spokesmen at the Phnom Penh conference made clear. We know that China's attitude, always hard, hardened even further (though late in January, the Chinese had apparently been willing to attend a new Geneva conference). Obviously if Hanoi, the NLF, and Peking, major forces in eventual negotiations, rejected peace proposals, no conference was possible. But, if these three were convinced that America was only acting out of desperation and if they in fact did not fear the destruction ensuing from air attacks, why should they not continue to press for negotiations?

Here we might do well to recall what happened in the

Korean War between the time negotiations first began and two years later when the armistice was signed at Panmunjom: the war continued both on land and in the air—North Korea was devastated by American air power, and Chinese and North Korean armies sustained tremendous losses in the land battles that went on continuously. It is probable that the NLF, Hanoi, and Peking, with the Korean experience as their model, concluded that America was determined to pursue the war, with increased air attacks on the North and increased infusion of men and equipment into the South, even while negotiations were going on. In such a case, Hanoi and the NLF would have faced the danger of lowering the morale of their peoples by conjuring up false possibilities of peace through negotiation.

Moreover, and perhaps even more significantly, the NLF remembered what had happened at Geneva, when Moscow, Peking, and Ho Chi Minh agreed to the partition of the country, requiring the Cochin-Chinese Vietminh to surrender large tracts of territory they had won from the French. The Vietcong guerrillas would have regarded agreement to negotiate on the part of Hanoi and NLF leaders, in the face of increasing American commitment to the fight, as a sign of weakness, and even worse, as a sign of a second possible betrayal. Thus, faced with increasing American pressure, Hanoi and the NLF had reason for their choice to fight back.

If escalation thus blocked international moves toward peace, how did it operate to strengthen the commitment of the South Vietnamese government to continue the fight? One of the justifications for U.S. escalation most often repeated by American officials is that it helps to raise the morale of the South Vietnamese. Raising morale can only mean strengthening the hand of the right-wing, hard-line forces, which were, at this time, those surrounding Thieu.

Several reports from South Vietnam have spoken of basic divisions within the South Vietnamese military, notably among left, right, and center forces. The events of the spring of 1966, notably the conflict between Thi and Ky, suggest the correctness of this analysis. We do not know how the American Embassy in Saigon operates within the battle lines of South Vietnamese politics, though we have seen reports that during every coup, American officials and officers are in contact with the leading elements.

We would suggest that every American escalation of the war has given a moral and material shot-in-the-arm to precisely those elements, namely the right-wing, in the South Vietnamese government who were committed to the fight against the Vietcong. It seems as if every time the pro-Thi and potentially neutralist forces acquired a new chess piece from the Buddhists, *e. g.*, through demonstrations, the pro-Thieu forces received, in return, a counterpiece from the United States.

V

"Four Points" or "Unconditional Discussions": Massive Escalation (March—April 1965)

SUMMARY: As the pace of the war increased in the first seven months of 1965, the sense of "crisis" became more or less continuous, with recurring manifestations of war-weariness in Saigon, negotiations offers from various sources (especially in February and March), and a steady increase of the U.S. war effort in South Vietnam. One can discern in this period three focal decisions by Washington after direct consultations with U.S. authorities in Saigon: the bombing of North Vietnam on February 7, the decision to double U.S. troops at the time of President Johnson's "unconditional discussions" speech on April 7, and the further doubling announced by his speech of July 28. The same period also saw a gradual increase in the United States' willingness to negotiate, provided always that negotiations were from a position of relative strength, to achieve an "honorable" peace.

In early March, the Chinese violently attacked the notion of considering negotiations before the total withdrawal of U.S. troops. At this time, the Chinese position was publicly endorsed (to the great disappointment of Prince Sihanouk) by both North Vietnam and especially the NLF. Later in March, there were signs that North Vietnam (if not also the NLF) might agree after all to negotiate on certain conditions, such as an end to escalation, and a commitment ultimately to withdraw. These signs were confirmed by North Vietnam's "four points" of April 8, which (in contrast to the Chinese position) publicly envisaged a Geneva-type conference follow-

ing "recognition" of certain "rights." But these conditions were publicly rejected by President Johnson in his speech of April 7, while his counteroffer of "unconditional discussions" (which in fact did entail certain conditions) had no chance of interesting the other side and had in fact already been rejected publicly by them. Although Johnson's new statement of policy on April 7 was undoubtedly more moderate than what many spokesmen in the Pentagon had been calling for, it rejected what was in fact a significant and viable feeler from North Vietnam, and thus decreased rather than increased the chance of negotiations. More specifically, the chance of unconditional discussions ever taking place had, as was suggested by international leaders at the time, been virtually eliminated by the rapid escalation which was just taking place against North Vietnam.

To understand the pressures on the United States at this time to negotiate, it is necessary to recall the proposal of President de Gaulle on February 23 for negotiations without preconditions, the supporting plea of U Thant on February 24, and Kosygin's statement on February 26:

> The friends of peace ask for a strict application of the Geneva Accords in order to prevent an escalation of the conflict to all of Southeast Asia and to find at a conference table the measures permitting a solution of the Indo-Chinese problems. It is necessary first and above all that the United States end their acts of aggression against the DRV in order to create conditions for exploring ways conducive to normalization of the situation in Indo-China (*LM*, March 3, 1965, p. 1).[1]

These appeals met with a discouraging response from two directions. On the one hand, the United States continued a slow but systematic expansion of the war. On February 24, U.S. jets were publicly used for the first time in air strikes against the NLF. On March 2, the United States and South Vietnam conducted the first explicitly nonretaliatory raid

[1] *Le Monde* attached considerable importance to this statement as the first public allusion from the U.S.S.R. to a conference not limited to Cambodia or Laos.

against North Vietnam (*NYT*, March 3, 1965, p. 1).[2] On March 7, 3,500 U.S. Marines were sent ashore at Danang, albeit with firm assurances from Dean Rusk that "It is not their mission to engage in the pacification operations."

> Well, as a matter of fact the South Vietnamese themselves have felt that ground combat personnel is not what is needed. They have very substantial armed forces that are fighting with effectiveness and with gallantry. . . . The South Vietnamese Government has not asked for international ground forces to support their effort.[3]

Dean Rusk, on February 25 and again on March 12, suggested that there was no indication that the French proposal for negotiations "might have some chance of success." According to his doctrine of the "Missing Piece," what was needed was substantial indication that "Hanoi is prepared to stop doing what it is doing against its neighbors" (*Dept. of State Bulletin*, March 15, 1965, pp. 364-370).

But the response from Chinese quarters was equally intransigent, and this fact had its consequences at a series of international conferences which took place during March. During the first week in March, there took place in Moscow the meeting of nineteen Communist Parties which had originally been scheduled by Khrushchev as a Conference but was now drastically scaled down by his successors to a "con-

[2] The *Times* report stated: "The attacks followed by a day a declaration by Premier Phan Huy Quat that there could be no peace until the 'Communists end the war they have provoked and stop their infiltration.' The Premier spoke out as talk of peace through negotiations was increasing in Saigon." The attacks were somewhat ironic in view of the previous leak that President Johnson had authorized "a continuing, limited air war against North Vietnam to bring about a negotiated settlement of the Vietnam problem on honorable terms" (*NYT* (from Saigon), March 1, 1965, p. 9). According to this report, the plan called for using only a few planes; the 160 planes used during February were too many. The attacks on March 3, as it happened, also used exactly 160 planes.

[3] Dean Rusk on "Face the Nation," March 7 (*Dept of State Bulletin*, March 29, 1965, pp. 442-443). On February 25, the Secretary had given equally misleading assurances with respect to the ROK contingent: "Well, the South Korean personnel that are going into South Vietnam are not going there for combat purposes. They will be primarily engaged, I understand, on engineering tasks here and there" (*Dept. of State Bulletin*, March 15, 1965, p. 370).

sultative meeting." Neither the North Vietnamese Party nor the more conspicuously pro-Chinese parties attended. A major attack by the Chinese on Russian "Khrushchevism without Khrushchev" was timed to coincide with the opening of this meeting; and the famous attack on the U.S. Embassy in Moscow followed three days later. Since then the Chinese have been demanding that the Soviet leaders admit that the decision to convene the conference was "wrong and illegal" (*Peking Review*, April, 1966, p. 6).

On March 4, the Chinese government released a statement calling for immediate United States withdrawal as the "sole way out," its equivalent of Secretary Rusk's "Missing Piece" doctrine.

> There is indeed an honorable way out for the United States, that is, to admit its mistakes without delay, immediately stop its armed intervention and aggression in Vietnam, and immediately withdraw all its armed forces from South Vietnam in accordance with the 1954 Geneva Agreements. This is the only way for the United States to save its face, and there is no other way out (FBIS *Daily Report,* March 5, 1965, BBB7).

An editorial the next day in Hanoi's newspaper *Nhan Dan* seemed hardly less intransigent:

> The only way for them is to end their policy of aggression and intervention, withdraw all their troops, military personnel and war means from South Vietnam, respect the Geneva Agreements, and let the Vietnamese people settle their internal affairs by themselves (FBIS *Daily Report,* March 5, 1965, JJJ2).[4]

In this context it is hardly surprising that the Moscow meeting failed to develop in any way the earlier Russian allusions to a political settlement in Vietnam. Although no proposal concerning Vietnam was contained in the final communiqué of the meeting, it was reported by Tass on March 11 that

[4] The "sole way out" doctrine was repeated by Hanoi Radio as late as March 30: "The only way out for them to end their disastrous failures . . . has been mapped out by our people—that path is the withdrawal of the U. S. Army from South Vietnam."

> In the name of their parties, the participants of the meeting demanded an immediate withdrawal of U.S. armed forces and their satellites from South Vietnam and the cessation of military attacks against the DRV (FBIS *Daily Report*, March 12, 1965, BB3).

The evident failure of the pro-Soviet parties to reach a strong common line with regard to China was viewed by western observers in Moscow, according to *The New York Times*,

> as the most telling evidence of the decline of the authority of the Soviet Communist leadership over foreign parties (*NYT*, March 10, 1965, p. 6).

Others at this time thought that Soviet influence in the Communist bloc seemed to have sunk lower than ever before, partly because of increasing U.S. intransigence in Vietnam and the Russian failure to respond to it. We now know, from an extremely candid Chinese account of Soviet-Chinese differences (in Peking *People's Daily*, November 11, 1965), that the Chinese insisted on U.S. troop withdrawal from Vietnam, whereas the Soviet Union was pressing for negotiations following an end to U.S. attacks on North Vietnam. According to a Chinese Government Declaration of March 12, a complete withdrawal of U.S. troops was "the sole and unique possible solution for a political settlement of the Vietnamese question" (*LM*, March 14-15, p. 2).

The long shadow of Chinese influence could be detected at the Indo-Chinese Peoples' Conference which met in Phnom Penh March 1-9, 1965. In a speech scheduled for delivery, Prince Sihanouk envisaged a de Gaulle-like solution of a Geneva-type conference leading to the "real neutralization" of Indo-China (*LM*, February 28, 1965, p. 2).[5] Prince Sihanouk had clearly hoped that the Conference would endorse this proposal. However, the Conference had to be postponed from its original date of February 25 when the NLF and DRV delegations to the Conference proved unexpectedly rigid from the outset, objecting not only to Prince Sihanouk's agenda

[5] According to *Le Monde* on March 2, it was thought that the increasing peace demonstrations in Saigon made possible a "negotiated solution of the conflict."

but also to the presence of a Vietnamese neutralist delegation composed of exiles in Cambodia.

The opposition of the NLF delegation, revealed after the Conference received a bitterly anti-American message from Chou En-lai, was based on the fear that negotiations at Geneva would lead to a Laotian-type compromise, which would see the installation in Saigon of a so-called government of national union, in which there would coexist the NLF, the pro-American military right, and neutralist elements (*LM*, February 27, 1965, p. 2).

On March 8, Sihanouk was reported as saying, "The Communists no longer want neutralization for South Vietnam—they demand the unconditional withdrawal of the Americans" (*LM*, March 9, 1965, p. 1). According to Georges Chaffard, a split had developed at the Conference between the Communists and the neutralists, Cambodian and other. The NLF and DRV delegations were both opposed to talk of a Geneva Conference, even if a more conciliatory spirit lurked behind their public intransigence (*LM*, March 5, 1965, p. 9). The resolution finally passed by the Conference called rather for U.S. withdrawal.

Meanwhile, the problems of Kosygin and Brezhnev in their country and in the bloc were being viewed with increasing concern by Tito. A *New York Times* article described the fear among Belgrade observers of a more militant Soviet line, or alternatively, of new and more militant Soviet leaders. Thus Tito wrote to President Johnson on March 2, urging him to "hold negotiations without preconditions from either side" (FBIS *Daily Report*, March 19, 1965, JJJ2).[6] In collaboration with Ben Bella of Algeria, he also arranged for a conference of ten (ultimately of seventeen) nonaligned nations in Belgrade, from March 13 to 15, 1965.[7]

As a result, seventeen neutral nations circulated (secretly at first)

[6] Johnson's reply at this time was in accordance with the "Missing Piece" doctrine: negotiations were possible only if "Hanoi shows itself willing to leave its neighbors alone" (*NYT*, March 14, 1965, p. 2).

[7] The ten original nations were Algeria, Ceylon, Cuba, Ethiopia, Ghana, India, Mali, Tunisia, the United Arab Republic, and Yugoslavia. Cuba and Mali ultimately declined to sign the appeal. It was, however, also signed by Afghanistan, Cyprus, Guinea, Iraq, Kenya, Nepal, Syria, Uganda, and Zambia.

> an urgent appeal to the parties concerned to start . . . negotiations, as soon as possible, without posing any preconditions, so that a political solution to the problem of Vietnam may be found in accordance with the legitimate aspirations of the Vietnamese people and in the spirit of the Geneva Agreements (*Current History*, October 1965, p. 237).

In view of the broad spectrum of neutrals who joined in this appeal, it is significant that Hanoi at this time attacked Tito. An important editorial in *Nhan Dan* for March 18 discussed Tito's letter to President Johnson and alleged that the March 4 issue of *Politika* in Belgrade had praised the United States for its willingness to consider negotiations.

> Tito has thus played the role of a stool pigeon of the United States in this peace fraud. . . . The allegation about negotiations without preconditions is itself a big bluff. . . . To solve the South Vietnam problem, the aggressor, who is U.S. imperialism, must end his aggressive war and withdraw all troops from South Vietnam. Without these conditions, no question can be solved. . . . There can be no question of negotiating with American imperialism at a time when it openly declares and brazenly steps up the war of aggression in South Vietnam and extends this war to North Vietnam. . . . By imploring a political solution to the Vietnam problem from the Johnson clique, Tito also attempts to use the banner of false peace to win some political influence to his clique. This is a vicious act which is designed to lend a hand to the U.S. imperialists (FBIS *Daily Report*, March 19, JJJ2; March 24, BBB9, JJJ1l).

The last reference to Tito's "clique" reflects China's contest with Titoist neutralism for influence in Africa, at the time of Chou En-lai's impending visit to African nations and preparations for the June Afro-Asian Conference in Algiers. It is hardly surprising that Peking should have given prominence to this editorial in its own press, or that it took the unusual step of rebroadcasting it back to Vietnam two days later. The accession of Hanoi to the Peking position on negotiations seemed to be explicit and complete.[8]

[8] One possible nuance of difference lies in the allusion to the

The *Nhan Dan* editorial of March 18 is also significant for its explicit rejection of the Titoist formula of negotiations without preconditions, and for the description of this initiative as part of the U.S. "peace fraud." [9] Thus, when President Johnson offered "unconditional discussions" on April 7, he might seem (as on previous occasions) to be making a safely unacceptable offer, one which had already been rejected publicly by Hanoi.[10] Consequently, his speech and the *Nhan Dan* editorial might seem to be equally intransigent and sterile manifestations of a meaningless propaganda war. We shall, however, suggest that what the April 7 speech rejected may have been more significant than what it proposed.

The NLF Five Points of March 22, 1965

The Chinese position that no negotiations should precede U.S. troop withdrawal was echoed in the lengthy and very militant "five points" statement of the National Liberation Front on March 22, 1965. The statement is worth studying closely inasmuch as the "five points" of the NLF and the "four points" of Hanoi still remain the negotiating position of the other side, which the U.S. rejects.

> The South Vietnam National Liberation Front once again asserts that the U. S. scheme to send to South

[9] In contrast, Hanoi's formal reply one month later to the appeal of the 17 nonaligned nations, broadcasted over Hanoi Radio on April 19, was more moderate: "The Vietnam News Agency is authorized to make the folowing statement: . . . any solution to the South Vietnam issue without the decisive voice of the NLFSV is impractical" (FBIS *Daily Report,* April 20, 1965, JJJ2).

[10] An earlier example of a safely unacceptable offer by President Johnson would be that of February 3, 1964, to consider the neutralization of South Vietnam in exchange for the neutralization of North Vietnam. This formula had just been specifically ridiculed in the January issue of the North Vietnamese journal *Hoc Tap* (San Francisco *Chronicle,* February 14, 1964).

---

impossibility of negotiations at a time of escalation. This might not at first seem especially significant. It is, however, remarkable that Peking broadcasted virtually the entire editorial except for the one short paragraph which contains this sentence (FBIS *Daily Report,* March 31, 1965, JJJ15).

> Vietnam more combat troops of the navy, ground, and air forces of the U.S. and its satellites, to conduct air strikes against North Vietnam and the Kingdom of Laos in an attempt to gain a 'position of strength' and compel the South Vietnam National Liberation Front and the South Vietnamese people to sell out their Fatherland in some negotiations with the U.S. is definitely only a daydream of the crazy men in politics and adventurists in the military field. The South Vietnamese people would like to tell the U.S. imperialists and their agents: at present the only way for the U.S. imperialists is to get out of South Vietnam. . . . All negotiations with the U.S. imperialists at this moment are utterly useless if they still *refuse to* withdraw from South Vietnam all their troops and all kinds of war materials and means and those of their satellite countries; if they still *refuse to* dismantle all their military bases in South Vietnam; if the traitors still surrender South Vietnamese peoples' sacred rights of independence and democracy to the U.S. imperialists and if the South Vietnam National Front for Liberation—the only genuine representative of the 14 million South Vietnamese people—does not have its decisive voice (Consulate General of the Democratic Republic of Vietnam in India, *Vietnam,* V, 32, (April 1965), p. 11; cf. M. Gettleman (ed.), *Vietnam: History, Documents and Opinions on a Major World Crisis*, p. 414; emphasis added).

These are the only references to negotiations in the statement. We have, however, quoted from the statement in the version released by North Vietnam, by Peking (with great fanfare) on March 25, and by Moscow. All of these texts were released via Hanoi March 23, and it may be that Hanoi had significantly toned down the NLF statement. The text circulated by the FBIS in this country, based on the CIA's monitoring of NLF CLANDESTINE radio on March 22, is more belligerent at various points throughout the text; and in our citations the crucial verb "refuse to" is not included:

> At present all negotiations are useless as long as the U.S. imperialists do not withdraw. . . . (FBIS *Daily Report,* March 24, 1965, KKK8; M. Raskin and B. Fall, *The Viet-Nam Reader,* p. 242).

It is because of the FBIS version that the U.S. press has hereafter repeated that both the NLF five points of March 22 and the subsequent Hanoi four points of April 8 "insisted that the Americans must pull out before a peace conference could be considered" (*NYT*, November 24, 1965, p. 1). However, if we carefully examine both versions in the context of the *Nhan Dan* editorial, we find a different emphasis: negotiations are temporarily ("at present") useless, at a time when the war is being expanded and extended to North Vietnam; *and* the United States must withdraw. No matter who is responsible for the altering of this crucial sentence, the discrepancy between the CIA and Hanoi versions has considerable diplomatic implications which should not have been ignored by U.S. policy-makers. It is certain, moreover, that subsequent NLF statements suggested that *agreement* to withdraw, not prior withdrawal, was the condition for a political settlement: "If the U.S. imperialists do not agree to withdraw . . . there can exist no contact with the U.S. imperialists" (NLF statement of September 25, 1965, as monitored by the CIA).[11]

All of this suggests that, as early as March 23, the other side (at least Hanoi) was considering the possibility of a formula for settlement, in which negotiations to implement the Geneva Agreements could follow a firm commitment by the United States to withdraw from South Vietnam. Such a possibility was hinted at much more explicitly by Hanoi's four-point statement of April 8.

Events Leading to Hanoi's Four Points of April 8, 1965

On March 19, the U.S.S.R. published a draft letter for the cochairmen of the 1954 Geneva Conference (itself and the UK) which contained none of its earlier hints at negotiations. Instead it proposed to

> call on the United States Government to stop at once its aggressive acts against the DRV, withdraw all its troops and weapons from South Vietnam, and let the

[11] A similar NLF statement of January 30, 1966 ("All negotiations with the U. S. imperialists at this moment are entirely useless if they still refuse to withdraw from South Vietnam.") was cited by Secretary Rusk as proof of their "negative, harsh and unyielding" response which necessitated an end to the January lull in bombing (*NYT*, February 1, 1966, p. 12).

> Vietnamese people decide their internal affairs by themselves (FBIS *Daily Report,* March 19, 1965, JJJ1).

This intransigent formula, with its unexplained emphasis on the *immediate* cessation of the war against North Vietnam, together with other conditions not so qualified, was also used at various times by Ho Chi Minh (e. g. April 10, August 14, 1965). The same formula was further articulated and endorsed by North Vietnam's letter of March 22 to the members of the 1954 Geneva Conference:

> to demand that the U. S. Government respect and correctly implement the 1954 Geneva Agreements on Vietnam, put an immediate end to its war acts against the DRV, withdraw from South Vietnam all arms, military personnel and troops of the United States and its satellites, and let the South Vietnamese people settle by themselves their own affairs. Such is the only correct way to settle the present South Vietnam problem and to contribute to the defense of peace in Indo-China and Southeast Asia (FBIS *Daily Report,* March 24, 1965, JJJ2).

Meanwhile, rumors of Hanoi's real interest in finding a formula to permit negotiations began again to circulate in the Western press, as they had the previous December. According to *Le Monde* of April 9, 1965, "It has been known for more than a month that Mr. Ho and his men envisage a negotiated solution of the conflict."

On April 1, *The New York Times* reported from Moscow:

> Diplomats from a nonaligned country reported today that North Vietnamese officials had indicated that their Government might be willing to agree to a new Geneva conference on Indo-China. The diplomats made it clear that the position taken in private by Vietnamese officials appeared to be considerably more flexible than that taken publicly by the Hanoi regime. Publicly, Hanoi has said that negotiations on Vietnam could be started only if United States forces first withdrew from South Vietnam. No such condition was raised by the North Vietnamese officials in private conversations with the representatives of a neutral country, the source said. However, the North Vietnamese were quoted as having said

> also that the United States bombing attacks on North Vietnam were a blow to North Vietnam's prestige and had to be answered by counterblows against the Americans. . . . the North Vietnamese officials indicated that Hanoi was eager to avoid direct intervention on North Vietnam's soil by either the Russians or the Chinese (*NYT*, April 1, 1965, p. 1).

On the same day, William Warbey, left-wing British Labor M.P., reported in a letter to the London *Times* that he had seen Ho Chi Minh and Pham Van Dong "ten weeks ago," at which time they had spelled out "what they meant by the 'essentials of the Geneva Agreements.' " These included international recognition of the independence and unity of Vietnam, freedom from foreign intervention, a "democratic coalition" in South Vietnam, and the negotiation without interference of relations between North and South Vietnam by the Vietnamese themselves. This thumbnail sketch of the subsequent four points was accompanied by the same emphasis on the cessation of attacks, rather than troop withdrawal, as the necessary precondition for negotiations.[12]

In the light of the public intransigence of the DRV in Phnom Penh and of *Nhan Dan* on March 18, and also of private rumors thereafter, the very *nuancé* and balanced statement of Premier Pham Van Dong on April 8 appears to be highly significant. In brief, Pham Van Dong set forth four points as the basis for a political settlement, and added that recognition of this basis could lead to the reconvening of a Geneva-type conference. There was no mention of the NLF five points or of the insistence that the NLF, as the "sole genuine representative of the South Vietnamese people," be given a "decisive voice." The four points should be read in their entirety (see Appendix B) but may be summarized as follows. The first point states:

[12] "What then holds up a peace conference of interested parties, and the ending of the slaughter in Vietnam? North Vietnamese insistence on withdrawal of American forces from South Vietnam as a precondition of their participation in a Conference? No. Mr. Pham Van Dong was emphatic that this was *not* a precondition; it was, he said, a subject to be discussed and arranged at the Conference itself. The only precondition is a cease-fire; the Americans and the South Vietnamese Air Force must stop their attacks on North Vietnam" (London *Times*, April 1, 1965, p. 13).

> Recognition of the basic national rights of the Vietnamese people: peace, independence, sovereignty, unity, and territorial integrity (a quotation from the 1954 text). According to the Geneva Agreements, the U.S. Government must withdraw from Vietnam . . .

Under the same point, (i. e., *recognition* of basic national rights) the United States "must" dismantle all bases, cancel its military alliance and its intervention in South Vietnam and acts of war against North Vietnam.

The second point said that "pending the peaceful reunification of Vietnam," the military provisions of the 1954 Agreements must be "strictly respected: . . . there must be no foreign bases, troops and military personnel" in the two territories.

The third point called for the settlement of South Vietnam's internal affairs "by the South Vietnamese people themselves, in accordance with the program of the South Vietnam National Front for Liberation without any foreign interference." [13]

The fourth point excluded foreign interference in settling the eventual peaceful reunification of all Vietnam.

The four-point program was put forward as the DRV's policy of support for, and implementation of, the basic provisions of the 1954 Geneva Agreements. However, the Premier indicated a change in public policy by adding:

> The Government of the Democratic Republic of Vietnam is of the view that the above-expounded stand is the basis for the soundest political settlement of the Vietnam problem. *If this basis is recognized* (our emphasis), favorable conditions will be created for the settlement of the Vietnam problem, and it will be possible to consider the reconvening of an international conference along the platform of the 1954 Geneva Conference on Vietnam.

Given the time difference between Hanoi and Washington, this speech must have been delivered within a few hours of President Johnson's speech (called on very short notice) at

[13] In Rusk's letter of December 1965 to Premier Fanfani of Italy, this was the only one of the four points to which objection was raised, because of its reference to the NLF.

Johns Hopkins on April 7. When the text was belatedly released by Hanoi, on April 13, it contained a lengthy and detailed response to the Johns Hopkins speech. Specifically, the United States was attacked for refusing to recognize or obey the Geneva Agreements, as evidenced by the attempt to justify the division of Vietnam (see below). Particular attention was drawn to Johnson's statement "We will not withdraw, either openly or under the cloak of a meaningless agreement." Furthermore, the United States was attacked because "At present, they persistently refuse to reconvene the international conference on Cambodia and Laos (FBIS *Daily Report,* April 16, 1965, JJJ9). This timely reference to the old proposal for a Conference on Cambodia came just as it was formally revived by the U.S.S.R. (as cochairman) on April 8, after it had been endorsed by the French on March 25, and even by the Chinese on March 20.

On April 10, a top-level DRV delegation (Party Secretary Le Duan, General Vo Nguyen Giap, and pro-Peking Foreign Minister Nguyen Duy Trinh) left for a week in Moscow, without apparently spending any time in Peking. On April 17, a joint U.S.S.R.-DRV communiqué was released which repeated the substance of the four points, while calling for both U.S. troop withdrawal and an "immediate end" to U.S. actions against North Vietnam. While it called again for conferences on Laos and Cambodia, the communiqué failed to link the four points to a conference on Vietnam. Such a possibility was however raised by a *Nhan Dan* commentary on the communiqué two days later.

It has been suggested that, in releasing the four points, the North Vietnamese government decided to risk departing from the Peking line and to entertain the possibility of a Laotian formula for settlement, where U.S. agreement to withdraw, rather than actual withdrawal, could lead, together with a *de facto* reduction in hostilities, to negotiations. That such a decision was made at some point is evident from the public allusion to the Laotian settlement by Hanoi Radio on July 16, shortly before the July escalation (see below). The text of the four points themselves, with their emphasis on recognition rather than the fulfillment of demands, supports this interpretation. In recognizing the possibility of a Conference, Premier Pham Van Dong had clearly departed from the public position of his government one month earlier, and still further from the Chinese demand for immediate withdrawal.

Just how difficult and important was this change is indicated by a report published one day earlier:

> Premier Chou En-lai has sent word to U Thant, the Secretary-General, that any negotiations on peace in Vietnam must be undertaken directly with the Vietcong forces in South Vietnam and not with Communist China *or North Vietnam*. He thus rebuffed repeated suggestions by Mr. Thant for group negotiations (*NYT*, April 7, 1965, p. 1; emphasis added).

Inasmuch as in January 1966, the U.S. government's fourteen points came very close to a point by point "recognition" of most of the four points ("We do not desire to retain U.S. troops in South Vietnam after peace is assured"), it is disappointing that President Johnson did not even mention the existence of the four points until July 28, by which time the United States involvement in the war had enormously increased.[14] It is even more disappointing that the possibility of a Laotian formula had been substantially rejected in ringing terms, at almost the time that Pham Van Dong's speech was delivered.

Events Leading to President Johnson's "Unconditional Discussions" Speech of April 7, 1965.

In late February, the United States began its systematic heavy bombing in South Vietnam. In March, it slowly expanded its program of sustained bombing to the North, provoking *The New York Times* to comment editorially:

> Now the United States is trying to win in North Vietnam the war that was gradually being lost in South Vietnam (*NYT*, March 7, 1965, p. 8E).

Beginning about March 14 and lasting until about April 7, there was a very marked escalation in the area, nature, and above all the frequency of U.S. air attacks against North Viet-

[14] The first official recognition of the four points by the United States was in Dean Rusk's comment in May that they "do not go to the heart of the matter."

nam: the United States first moved gradually northward from the previously announced limit of the 19th parallel, bombed nonmilitary targets such as bridges, and adjusted to a schedule of daily raids (*NYT*, March 27, 1965, p. 2; March 29, p. 3; April 4, p. 1). About March 28, the U.S. Seventh Fleet began patrolling within the territorial waters of both South and North Vietnam; and Hanoi immediately responded with a charge that its coastal villages were being harassed (*LM*, April 1). In late March, both Russian and Chinese ships reported being intimidated or machine-gunned by U.S. planes in the Tonkin Gulf.

On March 27, Ambassador Taylor returned to Washington for consultations. (It should be noted that personal consultations by U.S. authorities in Washington and Saigon have preceded every major period of U.S. escalation discussed in this memorandum.) The Ambassador was well known as spokesman for a significantly intensified war, especially in the north; and some speculation was aroused by the President's failure to receive him before March 31 (*LM*, April 2, 1965, p. 2). All commentators agreed that a major increase in the United States commitment was being considered. According to Walter Lippman, writing on March 31, the Pentagon and the State Department had advised President Johnson to be ready to send 350,000 troops to South Vietnam, while advisers were said to be recommending the bombing of Haiphong and Hanoi.

It is true that at this time there were signs that the NLF forces were regrouping for more sustained operations in the central zone of Vietnam. It is true also that there were renewed signs of instability and nervousness in Saigon (as for example when the French language newspaper there was closed down on April 5 for an editorial "injurious to the war effort"). The fact remains that the chief overt acts of North Vietnam during this period seem to have been political rather than military. In this context, the sudden and rapid escalation of attacks against North Vietnam still needs to be explained.

Whether intentionally or not, the escalation seems to have had the effect of making negotiations unlikely. President Johnson again made it clear on April 1 that he did not think a Conference would be productive:

> At a time when international pressures on the United States are growing to begin negotiating a settlement of

> the war, Mr. Johnson made a point of stressing that there was no sign that the Communist powers were interested in negotiations. 'I have no indication and no evidence that they are ready and willing to negotiate under conditions that would be productive, and I know of no information we have received that would indicate any conference at this time would be productive or would hold out hopes of achieving . . . peace in the world,' Mr. Johnson said (*NYT*, April 2, 1965, p. 3).

This statement followed three events already discussed; the rumors from Moscow of Hanoi's willingness to negotiate, William Warbey's confirmation of this in his letter to the London *Times* and the appeal of the 17 nonaligned nations for negotiations without preconditions. This last had been published in Belgrade on April 1 and formally submitted to Secretary Rusk in Washington the same day. But the Belgrade newspaper *Borba*, when publishing the appeal, commented that in view of the recent U.S. escalation this proposal was probably no longer meaningful. As *Le Monde* reported on April 3:

> The nonaligned appeal has been published fifteen days after the conference of ambassadors, when the American bombings of North Vietnam are becoming systematic. In such circumstances, the Yugoslav commentators are letting it be understood since this morning that a cease-fire without preconditions would seem to have been bypassed by developments. 'In fifteen days, the situation has developed so rapidly that it would be unrealistic to believe that the negotiations could now have a chance of success,' writes *Borba*; 'one would have first of all to stop the aerial bombings of North Vietnam's territory and to cease using gas.'

Other international voices also linked the prospect of peace to an immediate *de facto* pause in the bombings. On March 26, Dobrynin reportedly told Secretary Rusk that the Soviet Union "could not do much to arrange a settlement in Vietnam until the United States stopped bombing North Vietnamese targets" (*NYT*, March 27, p. 2).

The Chinese attack on the Soviet Union in the Peking *People's Daily* (November 11, 1965), seems to confirm that the Soviet Union was pressing for a cessation of bombing as a prelude to negotiations:

> The new Soviet leadership, in a communication to several fraternal parties, clearly stated that the only condition they demanded for negotiations with the United States was the cessation of bombing attacks on North Vietnam. They furthermore indicated that they were seeking ways and means of resolving the Vietnam problem through the path of negotiations.

On April 2, the Canadian Prime Minister suggested publicly a "pause in the air strikes"; and President Johnson, it was reported, was "cool" to this plan (*NYT*, April 4).

In these circumstances, it is not clear that President Johnson had changed his mind about the unproductiveness of a Conference, when on very short notice he delivered his "unconditional discussions" speech at Johns Hopkins on April 7. Like his later speech of July 28, 1965, the speech combined the sword and the olive branch. On the one hand, the President for the first time tacitly dropped the earlier Rusk doctrine of the "missing piece" by no longer insisting on proof that Hanoi was prepared to stop its aggression. On the other hand, the "aggression" theory and the dangers of appeasement were emphasized as clearly as ever before.

> The central lesson of our time is that the appetite of aggression is never satisfied. To withdraw from one battlefield means only to prepare for the next. We must say in Southeast Asia—as we did in Europe—in the words of the Bible: 'Hitherto shalt thou come, but no further.' . . . Our objective is the independence of South Vietnam and its freedom from attack. . . . We will do everything necessary to reach that objective, and we will do only what is absolutely necessary. In recent months attacks on South Vietnam were stepped up. Thus it became necessary for us to increase our response and to make attacks by air. . . . We do this to slow down aggression. We do this to increase the confidence of the brave people of South Vietnam. . . . And we do this to convince the leaders of North Vietnam—and all who seek to share their conquest—of a simple fact: We will not be defeated. We will not grow tired. *We will not withdraw, either openly or under the cloak of a meaningless agreement* (emphasis added). We know that air attacks alone will not accomplish all of these purposes. But it is our best and prayerful judgment that they are a necessary part of the surest road to peace.

It will be seen that all three elements which had been bruited abroad as possible elements for a Laotian-type settlement were discussed in this passage only to be rejected. There was to be no tiring in the war effort. The air attacks on North Vietnam were specifically defended as necessary. And the refusal to withdraw was not only emphatic, but linked to the rejection of any "meaningless agreement." President Johnson seemed no more sympathetic to the Laotian formula than did the Chinese. It might even seem that the 1954 Geneva Agreement was equally unacceptable, inasmuch as the April 7 speech did not explicitly refer to it, and called instead for

> an independent South Vietnam—securely guaranteed and able to shape its own relationships to all others. . . . These are the essentials of any final settlement. . . . And we remain ready with this purpose for unconditional discussions.

As for the possibility of discussions with the NLF, this was explicitly rejected by Administration spokesmen at the time of the April 7 speech.[15] It was not known in this country at the time that the speech was followed by a particularly severe series of air raids on North Vietnam which both North Vietnam and Russia duly cited as evidence of Washington's insincerity (*NYT*, May 15, 1965, p. 1). A general indication of the changing nature of the war was given by President Johnson in his message to Congress on May 4, 1965 (*NYT*, May 5, 1965, p. 18):

> In February, we flew 160 strike sorties against military targets in North Vietnam. In April, we flew over 1,500 strike sorties against such targets. Prior to mid-February,

[15] Nor was there any indication of a change in American policy in the thousands of leaflets scattered over North Vietnam by American planes shortly after the speech. The leaflet set forth the South Vietnamese position. The National Liberation Front would be debarred from all negotiation, since it is "only an instrument created by the Communist North Vietnamese." It also declared that negotiations could take place only after "preconditions (such as the withdrawal of Communist troops and cadres) laid out by the Republic of Vietnam during eventual preliminary talks will have been accepted and carried out." This withdrawal was further specified as meaning "previous withdrawal of the Vietcong armed units and political cadres" as well as those of the North Vietnamese.

> we flew no strike sorties inside South Vietnam. In March and April, we flew more than 3,200 strike sorties against military targets in hostile areas inside the country.

President Johnson followed up with a singular statement at his press conference on the 27th:

> We have made every effort possible to find a peaceful solution. . . . America has not changed her essential position, and that purpose is peaceful settlement. That purpose is to resist aggression. That purpose is to avoid a wider war (*NYT*, April 28). [16]

The most striking feature of the April 7 speech, however, did not become clear until some months later. The month of March had seen only one major debarkation of 3,500 U.S. troops in South Vietnam; in the month after the April 7 speech, U.S. troops were augmented by 15,000 men, and by early August the U.S. troop commitment had reached 125,000 men. Secretary McNamara referred with pride to the unprecedented achievement of transporting 100,000 men 10,000 miles in the period of four months. And in this same period, it finally became clear that this was a U.S. war with the key role now taken directly by U.S. forces. This buildup

[16] This statement was passed over in silence by third parties and others who had worked for negotiations in the past year, and been rebuffed by the United States.

It was the statements in July and August by Johnson that brought the leaks of the behind-the-scenes attempts to get the U.S. to negotiate. This came as Johnson extended the American statements of April:

"I must say that candor compels me to tell you that there has not been the slightest indication that the other side is interested in negotiation or in unconditional discussion, although the United States has made some dozen separate attempts to bring this about."

And on August 3:

"In 20 months we have agreed to fifteen different approaches to try to bring peace, and each of them has been turned down by the other side."

The latter was too bald for someone at the United Nations. This person, probably close to Stevenson, called in two correspondents and leaked the story that the United States had turned down secret talks with North Vietnam in the past fall which had been arranged by U Thant (*New York Herald-Tribune*, August 8, and Manchester *Guardian*, August 9).

had been predicted in quite accurate details by a *New York Times* correspondent on April 2, as the decision made by the Administration on that day (*NYT*, April 3, p. 1). The April 7 speech not only announced the U.S. commitment to "do everything necessary," but it also gave what is probably a quite candid account of its true motive for such a major decision.

> Over this war—and all Asia—is another reality: the deepening shadow of Communist China. The rulers in Hanoi are urged on by Peiping. This is a regime which has destroyed freedom in Tibet, which has attacked India, and has been condemned by the United Nations for aggression in Korea. It is a nation which is helping the forces of violence in almost every continent. The contest in Vietnam is part of a wider pattern of aggressive purposes.

In this context, it is all the more ironic to recall that, by April 1965, it was already clear that Chinese military support for Hanoi was strictly limited. And it is all the more important to ask why the four-point basis for negotiations, with its significant divergence from the Chinese position, was not only ignored, but substantially rejected at almost the time it was made.

VI

The First Pause in the Bombing of North Vietnam (May 1965)

SUMMARY: Early in May, appeals mounted both abroad and in the United States for a halt to the bombing of North Vietnam for the sake of negotiations. On May 15, the Administration announced that a pause in bombing had begun two days previously for "operational" reasons. As was later revealed, Secretary Rusk had secretly informed Hanoi that the United States would be watching for "significant reductions" in armed actions on their part, as an indication of a desire for negotiations. A response from Hanoi confirming that they wished to negotiate on the basis of their four points without prior withdrawal of American troops was transmitted to Washington by France.

The six-day pause was terminated May 18, with the State Department expressing disappointment "at the fact that there was no reaction" from Hanoi. Secretary Rusk later revised this account, saying the pause was ended after "polemical rejection" from Hanoi.

As frustration with the American position built up, international and American pressures began to focus on a "pause" in the air raids on North Vietnam to give Hanoi an opportunity to demonstrate its willingness to negotiate. One of the first world leaders to call for such a pause was Canada's Prime Minister, Lester Pearson (*NYT*, April 4, 1965). His idea was echoed by a number of leaders in this country and abroad, including Senator J. W. Fulbright.

This public pressure was heightened when the nationwide Inter-University Committee for Debate on Foreign

Policy scheduled a "Teach-in" to take place simultaneously in Washington and on a hundred campuses around the country on May 15. This movement had grown up in reaction to the bombing attacks on the North.

On May 15, the Administration announced a temporary suspension of the bombings, stating that the reasons were only "operational"—that is, for military reconnaissance and damage assessment. The pause [1] had already been underway two days (*NYT*, May 15, 1965). On the 18th, the air attacks were resumed with an attack on petroleum storage areas at Phuqui (*NYT*, May 19, 1965). Robert McCloskey, spokesman for the State Department, described the Administration as "disappointed at the fact that there was no reaction" from North Vietnam during the pause (*Ibid.*).[2]

This lack of response gave enormous support to President Johnson, hard-pressed by critics at home and abroad. For the next six months, Washington pointed to the pause in bombing as positive proof of the good intentions of the United States, and the lack of interest of North Vietnam in a peaceful settlement.

Six months later, it was revealed that Secretary of State Dean Rusk had secretly transmitted a message to Hanoi at the time through the North Vietnamese Embassy in Moscow (*NYT*, December 30, 1965). The message said the pause was "for a period beginning at noon Washington time, Wednesday the 12th of May, and running into next week." It said the United States would be watching for "significant

[1] The pause in the bombing of North Vietnam consisted of precisely that: reconnaissance and even strafing flights were continued. Meanwhile, the number of sorties in South Vietnam actually increased. On May 15, 150 air missions were flown over South Vietnam, "despite appeals from Buddhist leaders for a one-day truce to mark the 2,509th anniversary of Buddha's birth" (*NYT*, May 16, 1965).

[2] Since McCloskey's claim was directly contradicted by Secretary Rusk in January 1966, we shall cite it a little more fully. Mr. McCloskey said, in reply to a question, that it would be "correct" to say that the Administration was "disappointed at the fact that there was no reaction" from North Vietnam during the suspension of the bombings: "We must assume that the other side was aware that the strikes had not been carried out for a number of days, and we have seen no reaction to that fact" (as quoted in *NYT*, May 19, 1965).

reductions" in attacks on the South [3] (St. L. *P-D*, December 11, 1965). In spite of the short interval of time, hardly long enough for the National Liberation Front and North Vietnam to agree and reply, a response did come from Hanoi. The day before the bombings were resumed, the government of North Vietnam contacted the French government and asked that Washington be informed that they were prepared to negotiate on the basis of the Four Points without prior withdrawal of American troops (*NYT*, November 18, 1965, AP in St. L. *P-D*, November 17, 1965 and *LM*, November 19, 1965). High-ranking French officials, while admitting that the offer was not transmitted until a few hours after the bombing resumed, expressed regret that the United States

[3] The text of the U. S. note was released by Hanoi radio on December 10, 1965, and is worth reprinting:

"The highest authority in this government has asked me to inform Hanoi that there will be no air attacks on North Vietnam for a period beginning at noon Washington time, Wednesday, 12 May, and running into next week. In this decision, the U.S. Government has taken account of repeated suggestions from various quarters, including public statements by Hanoi representatives, that there can be no progress toward peace while there are air attacks on North Vietnam. The U.S. Government remains convinced that the underlying cause of trouble in Southeast Asia is armed action against the people and government of South Vietnam by forces whose actions can be decisively affected from North Vietnam.

"The United States will be very watchful to see whether in this period of pause there are significant reductions in such armed actions by such forces. The United States must emphasize that the road toward the end of armed attacks against the people and government of Vietnam is the only road which will permit the government of Vietnam and the government of the United States to bring a permanent end to their air attacks on North Vietnam.

"In taking this action, the United States is well aware of the risk that a temporary suspension of these air attacks may be understood as an indication of weakness, and it is therefore necessary for me to point out that if this pause should be misunderstood in this fashion by any party, it would be necessary to demonstrate more clearly than ever after the pause ended that the United States is determined not to accept aggression without reply in Vietnam. Moreover, the United States must point out that the decision to end air attacks for this limited trial period is one which it must be free to reverse, if, at any time in coming days, there should be actions by the other side in Vietnam which required immediate reply.

"But my government is very hopeful that there will be no such misunderstanding and that this first pause in air attacks may meet with a response which will permit further and more extended suspension of this form of military action in expectation of equal constructive actions by the other side in the future."

did not again halt the bombing when the message was received (*NYT*, November 19, 1965).[4]

Six months later, in November, the State Department confirmed that North Vietnam had, indeed, responded through the French (*NYT*, November 18, 1965). This was to widen the "credibility gap" between the White House and Congressional and other critics of the Vietnam policy.

The credibility gap became still greater when the Administration totally reversed its earlier story that there had been "no reaction" to the May pause. On January 21, Secretary Rusk said at a news conference that "In May, there was a cessation of bombing which ended *after* (emphasis added) a harsh rejection by the other side of any serious move toward peace" (*NYT*, January 22, 1966, p. 2). From this it would seem that the North Vietnamese message, instead of arriving too late, may actually have been the cause for the resumption of bombing. The Secretary's characteristic use of the word "serious" might imply that the note entertained a frivolous Communist move toward peace; but his next news conference ten days later, justifying the resumption of bombing on January 31, 1966, ruled out even this possibility: "A pause in the bombing last May had yielded only polemical rejection" (*NYT*, February 1, 1966, p. 12). Whatever the true story, it is certain that someone in the Administration misrepresented it.[5]

The May cessation of bombing demonstrated that de-escalation *could* produce the possibility for negotiation, while

[4] A slightly more alarming account, yet one credible in the light of Dean Rusk's testimony, is given by Jean Lacouture (*Vietnam: Between Two Truces*, pp. 282-283): "A Hanoi representative in an uncommitted capital announced that Dong's four points were not 'prior conditions' but general principles which, if accepted, would make the search for a settlement possible. A few hours later, however, the bombings were resumed, before the White House had been advised of the North Vietnamese diplomat's gesture."

[5] In the same January 31 news conference, Secretary Rusk assured the nation that "the details of time and place about contacts with particular capitals" were "the only point that I know of in which we have not given all of the detailed facts to the general public . . . there is no significant element here that has been withheld" (*NYT*, February 1, 1966). But if Mr. Rusk himself had not withheld information in January 1966, then his official spokesman, Mr. McCloskey, must have done so in May 1965.

the United States' previous political strategy of bombing North Vietnam into negotiations had had the opposite effect. Our government chose to overlook the lesson. Like Athens when it had an opportunity for a compromise peace with Sparta, "it strove for more" (Thucydides).

VII

New Ky Regime Given Further U. S. Support (July 1965)

SUMMARY: During the month of June, the United States began to take a more active and more independent role in an intensified war. On June 8, President Johnson first publicly authorized U.S. troops, formerly confined to patrolling, to search out the enemy; given South Vietnamese authorization (NYT, June 9, p. 1.) Meanwhile, there was speculation that Saigon's civilian regime, for some time accused of neutralist leanings, would not long survive:

"Phan Huy Quat has been so weakened by Roman Catholic opposition that he cannot survive as premier. . . . The United States mission's efforts have now begun to shift from helping to maintain Dr. Quat in power to paving the way for an orderly transfer of the premiership to someone else. . . . The Catholics are alleging that Dr. Quat lacks militancy and favors a neutralist solution to the Vietnam war" (NYT, June 9, pp. 1, 3).

On June 11, Saigon's last civilian government fell, and Air Vice-Marshal Ky became premier. There is no evidence that morale in South Vietnam's cities was improved as a result of this "orderly transfer." On June 30, Ky announced the temporary suspension of all 36 Vietnamese-language newspapers in Saigon, though 23 of these were allowed to resume publication on July 4 (NYT, July 1, p. 2; July 4, p. 1). On July 4, The New York Times reported that "Buddhist leaders had decided to bring down Major-General Nguyen Van Thieu, the chief of state" (p. 1), partly because of his Diemist (Can Lao Party) connections. Thich Tri Quang, militant Bud-

dhist leader, was "reported to have organized an anti-government campaign among his followers" (NYT, July 4, 1965, p. 7). On July 24, the military government announced that "support for neutralism" would henceforth be punishable by death (NYT, July 24, 1965, p. 2).[6]

The war was not going well either. Not only was the situation deteriorating in the countryside, so that the railway system was now admitted to be in a state of complete disintegration (LM, July 20, 1965), but acts of terrorism were increasing in the cities as well. In early July, the NLF published a proclamation warning South Vietnamese not to frequent restaurants and other public places where bombs might be thrown. As Mr. McNamara reported after his visit to Saigon in July, the situation was "serious, and in many areas it has deteriorated since my last visit 15 months ago."

This period is unlike all others discussed in this report in that there were indeed military developments to explain the increase in U.S. military involvement (from 75,000 to 125,000 troops) announced by President Johnson on July 28. What we wish to show, however, is that the President's announcement ignored significant diplomatic developments on the Communist side. As their military position improved, they talked more confidently of negotiations; their position of strength would appear to have made them more flexible, not less. Specifically, what had been transmitted secretly during the May "pause" in the bombing was now hinted at more and more openly: approval in principle of U.S. withdrawal (rather than withdrawal itself) was what was necessary for negotiations to begin. This clarification of the four points was obviously at odds with the Chinese position.[7]

[6] On the same day, 39 South Vietnamese army recruits jumped from a boat and drowned, in seeking to escape military service (*LM*, July 25-26, 1965).

[7] Some indication of the Peking attitude toward the four points may be gathered from the Peking broadcast of April 15, which gave each of the four points in full but entirely suppressed

During this period, the Sino-Soviet dispute was conducted more openly, with Hanoi apparently adhering more closely to the position of Moscow. The Chinese attack on the Russian position reached a climax at the World Peace Congress at Helsinki on July 11. The conference began with "procedural" difficulties between the Soviet Union on the one hand, and China, Albania, and North Korea on the other (*LM*, July 13, 1965). The division widened over a proposal in support of a cease-fire and negotiation, and the expedition of a mission from the Congress to all parties involved in Vietnam. The Chinese attacked the proposal, saying, "We can only negotiate the withdrawal of the American troops," and the Albanians accused the Russians of not wanting to term the United States "aggressors." The Russians walked out (*LM*, July 14, 1965). Ugandan Premier Obote reported that his talks with the Chinese indicated the United States must withdraw its troops before negotiations could take place (*LM*, July 19, 1965).

In the last week of July, the Chinese attack was violent. The Chinese paper *Ta Kung Pao* accused the Soviets of seeking only to "amass political capital" in Vietnam in order to negotiate with the United States from a more favorable position. They denounced this as a Soviet-American attempt to dominate the world (*LM*, July 27, 1965). From Tokyo, the Chinese said, "The Soviet Union is betraying the interests of the peoples of the entire world" (*LM*, July 29, 1965). Their charge of July 27 was vitriolic:

> They profess to be opposed to American imperialist aggression against Vietnam, but at the same time they embrace the faithful lackeys and the favorites of American imperialism, such as Shastri and Tito, sing in chorus with them and recommend negotiations to give a way out to American imperialism. (*LM*, July 29, 1965).

Meanwhile, Hanoi was publicly assuming positions that were strikingly divergent from those of Peking. The first

the following reference to the possibility of a conference (FBIS *Daily Report*, April 15, 1965, BBB4). An article in the Peking *People's Daily* of April 16, in approving the four points, stated that "The withdrawal of all U.S. armed forces is an indispensable *precondition* (rather than "basis") for the peaceful settlement of the Vietnamese question" (FBIS *Daily Report*, April 16, 1965, BBB1; emphasis added).

instance of this was its cautious response to a proposed peace mission of the British Commonwealth. Peking had contemptuously rejected the idea of such a mission, and so had the NLF. To be sure, the NLF's rejection of the British on June 27 may have been conditional, inasmuch as they again referred to the disputed wording of their March 22 Declaration:

> "It is necessary to declare once more that all negotiations with the imperialists are for the time being entirely useless, as long as they *refuse to* withdraw their troops. . . ." (*LM,* June 29, 1965; emphasis added).[8]

The response of Hanoi, however, was conspicuously different; officials there asked that the British message be readdressed to them as a "government," rather than as authorities. The North Vietnamese reply, according to officials in London

> indicated that it may receive the Commonwealth's peace mission if the mission's approaches reflect a formal recognition of it as a government. . . . Officials here . . . saw considerable significance in the entire tone of the North Vietnamese reply. . . . For the first time North Vietnam would have broken with the strong views of Peking. The assumption would be that Hanoi was acting with the approval and the encouragement of the Soviet government. In fact, there have been reports that Moscow was encouraging North Vietnam to admit the Commonwealth mission (*NYT,* July 1, 1965, p. 3).

This development did not go unheeded in Washington; one report said, "An authoritative State Department source . . . said that . . . it was the least negative pronouncement by Hanoi received since the Administration began putting out negotiation approaches" (*Ibid.*). Despite the official recognition of Hanoi's moderate attitude, no corresponding conces-

[8] As before, this is the NLF statement as reported in Hanoi. The CIA claims to have monitored the more militant and pro-Peking version over NLF clandestine radio: "It is necessary to state once more that under the present circumstances all negotiations with the U.S. imperialists are useless so long as the U.S. imperialists *do not* withdraw all their troops. . . ." (FBIS *Daily Report,* July 1, KKK3). If the CIA version of the text is accepted, then Hanoi's moderation, its pro-Russian stance and divergence from its other allies are even more striking.

sion came from either the British or the American governments.

On June 27 came the first clear indication that the NLF, as well as Hanoi, would consider a political agreement prior to the actual withdrawal of U.S. troops. On that day, the *London Sunday Times* quoted NLF President Nguyen Huu Tho as saying that "withdrawal of all American troops with all their arms and equipment" need only be the "basis of any eventual agreements" (*Nation,* September 6, 1965). The same position was reported by an ex-director of the American aid program in South Vietnam after an interview with the DRV Counselor in Algiers: Robert Browne noted, ". . . the North Vietnamese . . . demanded United States agreement in principle on a withdrawal of forces from Vietnam and not an actual withdrawal, as a precondition for negotiations" (*NYT,* July 22, 1965, p. 3). Finally an official statement of this position came in an article by a leading North Vietnamese defense spokesman, Nguyen Van Vinh, broadcasted over Radio Hanoi on July 16. After reiterating the March 22 and April 8 positions, he said:

> . . . to have a political solution and to achieve true peace in South Vietnam, first of all the United States imperialists must approve the withdrawal of their forces. Concerning the way of conducting this withdrawal, the imperialist side has had much experience; the French have withdrawn from Indo-China and Algeria, and the Americans have withdrawn from Laos and other areas in the world. (FBIS *Daily Report,* July 22, 1965 JJJ7).

Vinh's three examples seem to have been carefully selected. In each case the withdrawal of troops was subsequent to the conference and the agreement. In Laos, for example, a declaration was signed June 21, 1962, but United States troops were not to be withdrawn until October 7, 1962. Vinh's statement was thus a public confirmation that the four points would not entail a U.S. troop withdrawal prior to negotiations; nevertheless, it was not reported in the U.S. press, nor was a virtually identical broadcast of September 27, 1965.[9] Instead,

[9] "To attain a political solution and genuine peace in South Vietnam, the U.S. imperialists must first of all accept withdrawal of their troops. As for how this withdrawal will be carried out, the

as late as November, *The New York Times* reported that Hanoi's four points "insisted that the Americans must pull out before a peace conference could be considered" (*NYT*, November 24, 1965, p. 1). Hanoi had in fact made a public concession, by suggesting that the U.S. consider the type of general commitment to withdraw, a concession that the United States belatedly began to recognize and respond to in January 1966.[10]

In his major policy speech of July 28, President Johnson gave no such commitment. Repeating the untenable but customary claim that "there has been no answer" from "the other side," he replied to Hanoi's concession with an order for immediate major escalation: the increase of U.S. troop commitment in Vietnam by an additional 50,000, bringing the total commitment to date to about 125,000 men. The President's response was no more than confirmation of his July 10 press conference statement that there would be no limit on troops sent to General Westmoreland if he requested them.

The President's policy speech on July 28, 1965, was a mixed bag of promises and threats. One is almost persuaded by the rhetoric that the additional 50,000 American troops he was ordering to Vietnam were messengers of good will. Evidently responding to those critics of Administration policy who were pointing out the softening in Hanoi in regard to negotiations, he said:

We are ready now, as we always have been, to move from

[10] "We do not desire to retain U.S. troops in South Vietnam after peace is assured" (*Dept. of State Bulletin,* January 24, 1966: the eighth of the 14 points). The first hint of this revised U.S. position came in Senator Mansfield's speech of September 1: "There shall be a withdrawal of all foreign forces and bases throughout Vietnam, north and south, provided peace can be reestablished and provided the arrangements for peace include adequate international guarantees of noninterference, not only for Vietnam, but for Laos and Cambodia as well" (*Congressional Record,* September 1, 1965, p. 21739). Senator Mansfield claimed that "this point was underscored by Secretary McNamara on June 16," but Mr. McNamara seems to have made no specific commitment or reference to the withdrawal of troops.

imperialist camp has had a lot of experience, such as the withdrawal of French troops from Indo-China, and Algeria, and the withdrawal of the Americans from Laos and other parts of the world" (FBIS *Daily Report,* September 27, 1965, JJJ6).

> the battlefield to the conference table. I have stated publicly, and many times, again and again, America's willingness to begin unconditional discussions with any government at any place at any time. Fifteen efforts have been made to start these discussions with the help of 40 nations throughout the world, but there has been no answer.

Given the unequivocal official statement in the July 16 broadcast on Radio Hanoi (quoted above), it was becoming more and more difficult to determine what the President meant by an "answer." The President did, however, offer a new version of American objectives in Vietnam which represented a softening of the U.S. position. For the first time, he took public note of the fact that Hanoi had "set forth its own proposals," and he added, "We are ready to discuss their proposals and our proposals, and any proposals of any government (note here the exclusion of the NLF) whose people may be affected." Avoiding any mention of "an independent South Vietnam," which had been demanded earlier, he announced that the American objective was to insure

> that the people of South Vietnam shall have the right of choice, the right to shape their own destiny in free elections in the South, or throughout all Vietnam under supervision (Dept. of State Publ. 7937).

Hanoi was not impressed by either the promises or the threats of President Johnson. An official response came from Ho Chi Minh, who said that Johnson was fooling no one with his talks of negotiations, while he stepped up the war. "South Vietnam will unquestionably be liberated," Ho said, adding, "Both zones . . . will achieve national unification step by step, without any kind of foreign interference" (*Pravda*, July 31, 1965).[11]

[11] American reaction to the escalation during July included attacks on the Johnson policy by Senators Morse and McGovern, and a warning from Governor Hatfield of Oregon that the United States was risking World War Three (*LM*, July 27, 1965). The fears of many of the Administration's critics had also been expressed clearly by two other persons. Tran Van Minh, former South Vietnamese representative to UNESCO, warned against the "free Vietnam" myth, related, he said, to another myth—the necessity to fight Communism in "defense of the free world." There had been support in Vietnam for fighting Communism in 1954, he

said, but this had declined since 1960. He warned that if the present war continued, the NLF would grow increasingly dependent upon Hanoi, and Hanoi upon China (*LM*, July 11, 1965). At the same time, Robert Kennedy told the graduating class at the International Police Academy that "Response to revolutionary wars should be political in the beginning, political at the end, and political always." A suppressed statement in his text was "If, in response to revolutionary activity, a government can only promise its people ten years of napalm or heavy artillery, there will not be government for long" (*LM*, July 11, 1965).

VIII

The La Pira-Fanfani Overture (November—December 1965)

SUMMARY: Continuing United States military escalation had resulted by the fall of 1965 in deeper North Vietnamese involvement in South Vietnam and increasingly militant rhetoric from Hanoi. In October, the Hungarian Foreign Minister reported to the U.N. on his visit to Hanoi, appealing for an end to the bombing of North Vietnam. Despite increasing tensions within the Communist bloc, Hanoi Radio once again broadcasted a proposal for negotiations based on the four points, asking for U.S. acceptance of eventual withdrawal as in Laos. A series of revelations in November and December that the United States had rejected earlier peace feelers was met only with such Administration responses as that of President Johnson's characterization of Hanoi's attitude as "completely negative."

In mid-December, still another opportunity for negotiation was revealed. A news report, immediately confirmed by Goldberg, recounted a revised "basis" for negotiations reported by the Italian Professor La Pira after a conference with Ho Chi Minh in Hanoi. The proposal, transmitted by Italian Foreign Minister Fanfani to Secretary Rusk, asked for (a) a cease-fire, (b) "application . . . of the Geneva Accords," and possibly also (c) recognition of the NLF as a party to negotiations.

Administration response to this overture, it was revealed, had been to ask for clarification of terms. However, shortly after this message was transmitted to Hanoi, American planes bombed the Haiphong area. A warning that such an attack on either

Haiphong or Hanoi would make negotiations impossible had been received and recognized by the Administration. To many observers the attack seemed to be a reply to the La Pira-Fanfani overture.

In the fall, a number of forces combined to bring great pressure upon the American Government. One after another came appeals for peace from unexpected sources, leaks of American refusals to negotiate, growing Congressional and public criticism, and finally the "Fanfani" episode.

The American thesis was coming true, and still the Administration was on the defensive. In February, the thesis of the White Paper—that great help came from the North to support the Vietcong—was essentially untrue. Such aid as came to the Vietcong from the North was negligible. As the American military admitted at the time, more than eighty percent of Vietcong arms were captured American arms. The White Paper itself listed only 179 Communist weapons out of some 7,500 captured from the Vietcong over the 18-month period from June 1962 to January 1964 (Appendix D, of the White Paper). For 1963 and 1964, the White Paper estimated infiltration from the North at about 7,400 per year (Appendix C). It admitted that most of the infiltrators had been born in South Vietnam.

However, such a White Paper written a year later would have been on much sounder ground. By November of 1965, the infiltration rates from North Vietnam were approaching 4,500 men per month. The State Department said there were an estimated seven regiments of North Vietnamese troops in the South, where eight months before there was one (SD Concise History of Escalation, p. 3). Of course, even in these estimates, North Vietnamese account for only 20,000 of the 230,000 Vietcong forces. (The Mansfield Report estimate is only 14,000 of the 230,000.)

As the Mansfield Report points out, by November 1965, the intensity of the war had reached a new high. American troops had increased from 34,000 in May to 165,700 in November; there were 500,000 men in the South Vietnamese armed forces and 28,000 men from the Republic of Korea. The number of incidents initiated by the Vietcong rose steeply in the fall. According to the Senator's report: "The Vietcong initiated 1,038 incidents during the last week of November and the total number of incidents which had increased steadily throughout 1965 reached 3,588 in that month" (Mansfield Report, p. 3). The escalation of the war was bringing results. The North was supplying more and more support to the NLF. The NLF was more and more militant.

Many were concerned about the escalation of the war and the results it had brought. On the 4th of October, Pope Paul VI addressed the United Nations in New York, appealing for peace in Vietnam. His visit included meetings with President Johnson and Soviet Foreign Minister Gromyko (St. Louis *Post-Dispatch*, October 10, 1965). On October 6, Janos Peter, Hungarian Foreign Minister, spoke to the Geneva Assembly on the basis of his visit to Hanoi two months before. He reiterated the Russian thesis that

> a cessation of bombing of *North* Vietnam (emphasis added) was a necessary precondition to a peaceful settlement (*PD*, October 8, 1965).

In private conference with Secretary Rusk, Peter again urged that such a cessation would prove fruitful.[1] But the Conference between Rusk and Peter was followed by a State Department statement that Peter brought no "message from Hanoi."

Meanwhile, both Hanoi and the NLF gave evidence of their own reactions in public utterances. The escalation of the war was reflected in the increasingly intransigent statements coming out of Hanoi. On October 5, Pham Van Dong expounded his government's more stringent stand: as first indicated in a Foreign Office paper of September 23, the four points must now be not merely "recognized," but "accepted":

> The United States Government must solemnly declare its acceptance of this four-point stand before a political settlement of the Vietnam problem can be considered (FBIS *Daily Report*, October 6, 1965, JJJ1).[2]

[1] *NYT*, December 31, 1965, p. 2: "Many Communist diplomats have expressed their belief that a pause in the American bombing would ultimately bring about negotiations. . . . Janos Peter said as much to Secretary of State Dean Rusk."

[2] Mr. Rusk stated categorically on October 27 in Dallas: "Washington has not received any signals from Hanoi about what North Vietnam would do if the bombings ceased."

He spoke of a war that might last "five, ten, twenty years or longer if necessary." There were signs that the Sino-Soviet disagreement over negotiations was producing severe tensions, not only within the bloc, but inside North Vietnam itself. For example (after visiting Rumania and East Germany), a Vietnamese Workers' Party Delegation headed by Le Duc Tho signed in Paris with the French Communist Party a communiqué calling for "immediate withdrawal" of U.S. troops. On the other hand, Radio Hanoi broadcasted a second article by leading defense spokesman Nguyen Van Vinh (like that of July 16), demanding only acceptance of withdrawal: "to attain a political solution, . . . the U.S. imperialists must first of all *accept* withdrawal of their troops" (FBIS *Daily Report,* September 27, 1965, JJJ6; *vide supra*). He again referred to the examples of Indo-China in 1954, Algeria, and Laos, where private discussions and ultimately negotiations had preceded the withdrawal of troops. "If the U.S. imperialists accept the above stand of the people in both zones," he added, "we shall be ready to come to the conference table." He also warned ominously that if the United States still refused to withdraw, the South Vietnamese forces in North Vietnam "will return to South Vietnam." [3]

In the middle of a militant statement of September 25, the NLF gave further evidence that they, too, were looking for a United States agreement to withdraw:

> If the U.S. imperialists do not *agree to* withdraw . . . there can exist no contact with the U.S. imperialists (FBIS *Daily Report,* October 15, 1965; emphasis added).[4]

Prince Sihanouk, on the other hand, visited China in mid-

[3] It is significant that, in March 1966, the NLF and DRV (unlike pro-Chinese parties such as the New Zealand Communists, and even fence-sitters such as the Japanese Communists) both sent representatives to the 23rd Congress of the CPSU in Moscow.

[4] Radio Prague, one month later, reported that the NLF representative in Moscow, Nguyen Van Dong, had stated that the NLF did not demand U.S. troop withdrawal as a condition for negotiations, but only recognition of the NLF. He was alleged to have spoken also of strained relations between the NLF and China concerning the means of ending the war (*LM,* October 24-25, 1965). The story was, however, promptly denied by the NLF representative (*LM,* October 28, October 31 to November 1, 1965).

October; on leaving the country, in Rangoon on October 16, he denounced the Soviet Union for the "deliberate affront" of having cancelled an invitation to visit Russia in November (*LM*, October 17-18, 1965). The U.S. Air Force had just chosen this occasion to bomb Cambodia (on October 15); and on October 17 in Phnom Penh, Prince Sihanouk declared, "I am opposed to any reconciliation or compromise with the imperialists" (FBIS *Daily Report*, October 19, 1965). Still further tensions meanwhile had arisen between China and Algeria with respect to the proposed resumption of the Afro-Asian Conference in Algiers, which China opposed.

In short, the scene in the Communist camp was one of somewhat increased militancy, confusion, and political tensions which the United States totally failed to exploit. Superficially it might seem that in the fall of 1965 the other side was thus no less guilty than the United States for the continuance of the war, inasmuch as each side insisted intransigently on its own formula for approaching a political settlement. There was, however, this striking difference: the formula of the DRV four points was essentially compatible with the 1954 Geneva Agreements, while the objectives of the United States ("free elections" concerning South Vietnam's future, to be arranged by a dictatorial Saigon regime in the presence of foreign troops) were not. The Hanoi paper *Nhan Dan* could still claim with justice on September 24:

> While clamoring for peace and negotiations, the U.S. ruling circles have never spoken of the withdrawal of American troops from South Vietnam and the recognition of the fundamental national rights of the Vietnamese people as provided for in the 1954 Geneva Agreements (FBIS *Daily Report*, September 27, 1965, JJJ11).[5]

Furthermore, the United States had asked for a sign; and, on the crucial issue of U.S. troop withdrawal, an explicit and

[5] Senator Mansfield in his speech of September 1 had spoken of a "withdrawal of all foreign forces and bases throughout Vietnam, north and south" (*Congressional Record*, 1965, p. 21739); but this seemed to reflect the U.S. position that the Vietcong forces were "foreign" and should be withdrawn to North Vietnam before negotiations could begin. Nguyen Van Vinh, in the September 27 broadcast already cited, called it an "illusion" to expect withdrawal of the "South Vietnam Liberation Army, which they slanderously called North Vietnamese troops."

public concession had now been made by the North Vietnamese.

Throughout the fall, a series of forced disclosures by the Administration of rejected opportunities for peace talks added emphasis to increasing domestic pressures for negotiations. On the 15th of November, Robert McCloskey, State Department Press Officer, confirmed reports that the United States had rejected an offer by North Vietnam to meet in Rangoon, Burma, in September 1964 (*NYT*, November 16, 1965). The other efforts of Thant to arrange talks were also confirmed. On the 19th, McCloskey admitted that the North Vietnamese had attempted to open negotiations at the time of the May pause in bombing. He said the conditions offered then (the four points) were unacceptable to the American Government (*LM*, November 19, 1965). Background given reporters by the State Department explained that Rusk and his advisors thought that the Saigon Government was at a particularly low ebb in the fall of 1964 and that peace negotiations would endanger its survival. The fall of still another government at a critical moment in the war could be calculated to have disastrous results on the fighting, continued the off-the-record briefing (Marquis Childs, St. Louis *Post-Dispatch*, November 17, 1965). However, McCloskey's public explanation was: "On the basis of the total evidence available to us, we did not believe at any time that North Vietnam was prepared for serious peace talks" (*NYT*, November 16, 1965, p. 1).

However, the admissions of the approaches from North Vietnam brought strong reactions from members of the Senate Foreign Relations Committee. They said they had not been kept informed. Repeated statements by Administration officials, including the President, now looked false to the public, they said (St. Louis *Post-Dispatch*, November 26, 1965).

Senator Young (D-Ohio) returned from a Vietnam inspection to demand a five-day suspension in the bombing. He also attacked the role of the CIA in Vietnam as unnecessary and too active. *The New York Times* came out for suspension of the bombings (*LM*, November 21, 1965). The answer given by the Government to such appeals was that such a pause would be misinterpreted as a sign of weakness by North Vietnam and the Chinese (*NYT*, November 18, 1965).

In the wake of these revelations, Mr. Johnson and Mr. Rusk began giving great stress to the alleged intransigence and lack of response in Hanoi. On November 22, Secretary Rusk stated on television that messages from Hanoi contained "nothing in their substance that indicates a desire to conclude peace" (*LM*, November 23, 1965). On December 9, the President said:

> Our efforts to communicate our desire to talk about peace were met with silence from some, shrill propaganda from others. On the crucial question of readiness to meet without conditions, the response in Hanoi, and still more in Peking, remains completely negative (*NYT*, December 10, 1965, p. 13).

Secretary Rusk went even further:

> If Hanoi is saying that the United States Government must solemnly declare its recognition of their four-point stand and must prove this by practical deeds, and that includes, by the way, the point that the solution in South Vietnam must be the solution of the National Liberation Front, they say only then can a political solution be considered. . . . *We have never had any signal or sign from Hanoi* that their will is anything less than the imposition of their will on South Vietnam (*Ibid.*, emphasis added).

The third of Hanoi's four points, to which Mr. Rusk here alluded, states simply that

> 3. The internal affairs of South Vietnam must be settled by the South Vietnamese people themselves, in accordance with the program of the South Vietnam National Front for Liberation, without any foreign interference (see Appendix B).

Up to now, most observers had interpreted this to be an allusion to the NLF's political program of 1960: this called for the abolition of the existing Saigon regime, and its replacement, not by the NLF, but by a coalition government which would arrange for elections with universal suffrage.[6] Three weeks earlier, however, on November 20, the United

[6] Program of the National Liberation Front of South Vietnam, in Raskin and Fall, *The Viet-Nam Reader*, p. 216. On January 24, 1966, Ho Chi Minh was to speak of the NLF program which the U.S. should approve as one of independence, peace, democracy,

States had received an important communication which suggested that not even this minimal procedure need be "accepted." A promising signal *had* come from Hanoi.

On December 17, the St. Louis *Post-Dispatch* revealed a new peace message which Washington had received on November 20. It was based upon the four points. It had been delivered to Ambassador Goldberg by Italian Foreign Minister Fanfani and reported an interview between a Professor La Pira, Ho Chi Minh, and Pham Van Dong. The letter said that Ho Chi Minh and Premier Pham Van Dong had expressed a strong desire to find a peaceful solution. Ho wanted a cease-fire, a halt in the landing of American troops, and acceptance of the four points. He said the four points could "be reduced to a single point: application, in other words, of the Geneva Accords" (St. L. *P-D*, December 18, 1965).

The effect of this revelation was enormous. Immediately Ambassador Goldberg called a press conference to, in his words, head off a "crisis of confidence" in the Johnson Administration. Much was made of the damage caused by publication of the efforts going on behind the scenes. "We would have preferred to carry on this discussion in privacy," said Goldberg. Attempting to show that Washington had not dismissed the offer out of hand, he revealed that Secretary Rusk had replied through Fanfani to North Vietnam. He did not mention that the United States had waited two weeks to respond (St. L. *P-D*, December 20, 1965).

The American reply of December 4 said that it seemed North Vietnam's position was based on the Geneva Agreements without any qualifications or conditions. Continued Rusk, "We for our part would be willing to engage in negotiations on this basis without any qualifications or conditions." He disagreed that the four points were an authentic interpretation of the 1954 Agreements on the ground that "elements in the four points, notably the political program of the so-called National Liberation Front, have no basis in the Geneva Agreements."

> Hanoi's apparent insistence on a prior declaration accepting the four points thus appears both to be inconsistent with the agreements and to require a substantive condition to the negotiations.

---

neutrality, and an advance toward reunification "in the spirit of the 1954 Geneva Agreements" (*vide infra*).

> Nevertheless, we are prepared to include these four points for consideration in any peace talks along with any proposals which the United States, South Vietnam and other governments may wish to advance.

Rusk observed that the new information clarified that North Vietnam would not require prior withdrawal of American troops. He said that the United States was prepared for negotiations without a cease-fire. Further, any reduction or cessation of military activities would have to be reciprocal, while Hanoi's proposal placed no restraint on infiltration from the North (St. L. *P-D*, December 20, 1965).

As U Thant was pointing out at this very time, past overtures had failed because "bold steps" were needed in response and had not been forthcoming. While the letters were being passed, Mr. Thant was pleading that a reconvening of the Geneva Conference was the only means of restoring peace and stability:

> Even at this late hour—perhaps ten years too late—I still hold the view the Geneva Agreements can still be implemented. The only alternative to such a course is prolongation and escalation of the conflict resulting in appalling loss of life and tremendous destruction of property . . . the more the conflict is prolonged, the more complex and difficult will be the solution to the problem (*NYT*, November 17, 1965).

The American response came from Secretary Rusk. Secretary Rusk's letter of December 4 declined, in effect, to accept "application" of the 1954 Geneva Agreements, but expressed willingness "to engage in negotiations" on this basis. Inasmuch as the four points are very largely a reaffirmation of the principles of the 1954 Agreements, Mr. Rusk's objection to the third point seems to reiterate the substance of United States disagreement in 1954: namely, the United States was not willing to envisage a withdrawal of troops and the holding of elections "without any foreign interference." The most disappointing feature of Mr. Rusk's reply is his insistence on this bone of contention at a time when the other side was now for the first time apparently willing to forget about it. If, in fact, the United States was merely concerned to assure adequate guarantees for fair elections, it could certainly have agreed to the "application" of the Geneva Agreements, which had envisaged both free elections and an International Control Commission. If necessary, the United States could have insisted in negotiations that the latter be enlarged.

There are, however, very substantial grounds for thinking that Mr. Rusk did not want negotiations (and consequent elections) at this time, and again for the same reason that the United States was opposed to elections in 1956. To put it simply, the Vietcong was at this time a large force in control of most of the countryside; thus it was unlikely that either negotiations or elections would deprive them of a large share of influence in the postwar government. Mr. Rusk was to reiterate in a television interview on December 7 his position with regard to the NLF:

> Rusk said he would not consider making concessions to the NLF any more than anyone would consider rewarding a burglar who had broken into his house (St. L. *P-D*, December 20, 1965).

His refusal to contemplate rewards to the NLF helps us understand why the United States did not immediately accept (and might never have accepted) "application . . . of the Geneva Accords."

One disappointing feature of the United States reply is its gratuitous introduction of complications. Another is its date, at least two weeks after that of Mr. Fanfani's letter, and possibly longer still.[7] Although Professor La Pira's conversation with Ho Chi Minh took place on November 11, Mr. Rusk's reply was delivered to Mr. Fanfani in New York only on December 6. Mr. Fanfani summarized its observations in a document and, on December 13, he notified Mr. Rusk that this document had reached Hanoi. Two days later, on December 15, American planes bombed the Haiphong area for the first time, destroying a power station at Uong Bi, fourteen miles outside of Haiphong.

At the very best, this might seem like another gratuitous complication, and one with little military justification. The

[7] Mr. Fanfani's letter, as released by Washington, is dated "November 20"; yet it uses the expression "On Thursday" (without qualification) to date the interview which took place on Thursday, November 11. Mr. Rusk's reply is dated "December 4"; yet Mr. Fanfani in his reply of December 13 makes a point of specifying that he received it (in New York) on December 6.

credibility of U.S. seriousness about negotiations was weakened; inevitably "some U.N. delegates . . . pointed out that the war had been escalated after the United States reply was relayed to Hanoi" (San Francisco *Chronicle*, December 20, 1965, p. 11). Most people, however, did not know that on December 8 Ambassador Goldberg had been explicitly warned

> that Ho would not enter peace negotiations with the U.S. if the Hanoi-Haiphong area were bombed. (*PD*, December 29, 1965).

This information was transmitted to Mr. Goldberg in an interview and a 1,000-word memorandum by Peter Weiss, a New York lawyer who had also interviewed Professor La Pira for four hours on December 5. According to Barrett McGurn of the St. Louis *Post-Dispatch*:

> In Washington, Department of State sources confirmed last night that the Ho Chi Minh peace feeler as transmitted in the Weiss memorandum did "strongly intimate that the bombing of the Hanoi-Haiphong area would close the door on the possibility of a negotiated peace." Informed sources in Washington said that the North Vietnamese always had held that position, but that in the U.S. understanding of what the Communist regime meant by the Hanoi-Haiphong area, it had not been bombed yet. The informed sources did not disclose how they knew what the Communists meant by Hanoi-Haiphong (St. L. *P-D*, December 29, 1965).[8]

[8] The Weiss memorandum also claimed that Mr. Fanfani's first letter had omitted a second essential feature of Professor La Pira's message, namely that the NLF must be a party to negotiations (*PD*, December 20, 1965). This seems entirely plausible and much more consistent with the DRV position before and after than the Fanfani version, which implausibly omits all reference to the NLF. Thus the publication of the Fanfani version must have been quite embarrassing to Hanoi, and would explain Hanoi's denunciation of the reported feeler on December 18 as "sheer groundless fabrication" (*NYT*, December 19, p. 3). Yet even this denunciation echoed the central idea of the La Pira message in confirming that Ho Chi Minh and Pham Van Dong had "clearly explained the four-point stand of the Democratic Republic of Vietnam which illustrated the basic principles and provisions of the 1954 Agreements on Vietnam." According to Mr. Weiss, "All Mr. Fanfani had was a letter from Mr. La Pira, but what I had was four long hours of probing" (St. L. *P-D*, December 29, 1965).

The U.S. press paid little attention to this extraordinary story, yet it has never been denied.

With these revelations, President Johnson had a considerably larger "crisis of confidence" to head off. Diplomats in the UN considered the bombing of Haiphong "the real answer to the latest peace feeler by Hanoi." They found the Rusk reply "extremely disappointing." Concerning Goldberg's publication of the secret correspondence as proof of United States interest, at least one UN diplomat felt: "The best answer to the newspaper charge that Washington had rejected the peace feeler would have been the conclusion of peace in Vietnam" (St. L. *P-D*, December 20, 1965).

IX

The Second Pause in the Bombing of North Vietnam (December 24, 1965—January 31, 1966)

SUMMARY: Toward the end of 1965, President Johnson launched his "peace offensive." Leading American officials visited the capitals of several nations stating the American position. Rumors were rife about unofficial contacts between Washington and Hanoi, either directly or through third parties. Finally, early in January, the State Department released its fourteen points, which came closer to meeting the North Vietnamese position on all points except one: recognition of the NLF as an independent South Vietnamese political force, which therefore should participate in any negotiations. Within and outside the United States, many influential voices were raised urging Washington to concede this point. The essence of the North Vietnamese position was that (1) the United States should recognize the principles of the Geneva Accords (that is, recognize the principle of eventual withdrawal; (2) the United States should once and for all cease bombing North Vietnam; and (3) the United States should recognize the NLF. President Johnson had already accepted (1), and the pause in bombing indicated, at least, a tentative acceptance of (2); only (3) seemed unresolved.

However, what Washington conceded in words was not supported in actions. The bombing of the Uong Bi power plant in the vicinity of Haiphong, coming when the Fanfani-Rusk correspondence was revealed, had its counterpart in ground actions in South Vietnam. During the period of this bombing pause, a lull in ground fighting had set in. Though Vietcong incidents continued, newspapers reported the total absence of any clashes between North Vietnamese regulars and American forces, in sharp contrast to the situation only a few months before, as in the battle of the Iadrang Valley. However, Washington was not satisfied that Hanoi had begun to supply the "key signal" that Rusk had so often proclaimed he was waiting for. Just before the resumption of the bombing and soon after the short truce for Vietnamese New Year (Tet), United States forces launched in Central Vietnam the greatest amphibious offensive since the Inchon landing in Korea in 1950. The avowed aim of the operation was to search out North Vietnamese regulars and force them to fight.

The resumption of the bombing of North Vietnam and the great American offensive, coming at a time when signs of a gradual slowdown in the ground fighting were multiplying, and when the gap between the diplomatic positions of the two sides had narrowed, again destroyed the hope of ending the conflict. For the first time, pressure to prevent United States resumption of bombing and the widening of hostilities came not merely from the United Nations and foreign powers, but from a substantial body of opinion in America and particularly the United States Senate.

The so-called "peace offensive" of early 1966 and its alleged rejection by Hanoi are often cited as evidence that Washington's interest in negotiations surpasses that of the Communists. This "peace offensive" took place in the context of two separate and well-defined truces in the fighting:

a) A Christmas cease-fire among all parties (stemming from an NLF initiative, which after some reluctance the United States accepted and expanded): this began December 24 and was apparently quite successful.[1]

[1] "Despite a number of minor violations (20), the guerillas largely honored their own cease-fire declaration—from 7 P.M. Christmas Eve until 7 A.M. Christmas Day" (*NYT*, December 27, 1965, p. 1).

b) A Lunar New Year (Tet) cease-fire. Here, as before, there were two unilateral cease-fires. That of the NLF was proclaimed from 1 A.M. January 20 to 1 A.M. January 24, and regarded their South Vietnamese opponents only. That of the Saigon regime and American forces began eleven hours later and ended seven hours earlier. The NLF announced no cease-fire against "foreign" troops, and observed none. As a result it was widely reported in the U.S. press that Vietcong troops had violated the Lunar New Year cease-fire (*NYT*, January 22, 1966, p. 1); but *The New York Times* later reported that the NLF had observed the terms of its own cease-fire.

In the wake of the Christmas truce, it slowly became clear that U.S. bombings of North Vietnam had been suspended and not resumed. This "pause" in the bombing continued for thirty-seven days, from December 24, 1965 to January 31, 1966. Later the United States reported that, on December 29, through diplomatic channels in Burma, it had presented to the North Vietnamese a letter outlining American aims (*NYT*, January 15, 1966, p. 3). Just before New Year's, the Pope began corresponding with parties on both sides, and from January 7-13, Shelepin visited Hanoi. In early January, the State Department released its so-called "fourteen points," which came close (closer even than Senator Mansfield's important Senate speech on September 1, 1965) to meeting three of the four points outlined by Hanoi as a "basis" for a political settlement on April 8, 1965 (see Appendices A and B). These two developments increased the possibilities of a political settlement to the Vietnamese problem; and it seems quite possible that both Hanoi and the NLF likewise found them to be of interest, in view of the indisputable fact that, militarily speaking, January was "a relatively quiet month in which there was little contact with organized Vietcong guerilla units or with infiltrated North Vietnamese troops" (*NYT*, February 3, 1966, p.1). It is true that isolated guerilla incidents continued throughout this period, but the disciplined larger units of both the NLF and the DRV held their hand and refrained from fighting. Thus it is disappointing that the United States chose to end the truce of Tet with new offensives, seven hours before the truce of the NLF had expired.

Given the lull, United States behavior in the next seven days of the "pause" is even harder to explain. The United

States continued a rapid military buildup of its own forces, while continually citing a much smaller buildup on the other side as a major ground to justify resumption of bombing. On January 27, in Central Vietnam, it launched "Operation Masher," a huge search-and-destroy mission by both land and sea, involving "the largest amphibious operation by the United States Marines since the 1950 Inchon landing in Korea" (*NYT*, January 30, 1966, p. 1). The purpose of the offensive seems to have been to end the lull; as a brigade commander in the land operations put it:

> the plan is to move three infantry and three artillery battalions repeatedly across a 450 square-mile section of Bindinh Province *to look for* a battle (*NYT*, January 28, 1966, p. 12; emphasis added).

On January 28, on a sandy beach near Anthai, 300 U.S. First Cavalrymen encountered some 500 guerillas and killed 103 of them in a two-day battle. Some of the dead were "dressed in the khaki uniform of the North Vietnamese Army" (*NYT*, January 29, 1966, p. 1; cf. January 30, p. 1); and on January 30, the Americans said that these "had been identified as members of the 18th Regiment of the 325th North Vietnamese Division" (*NYT*, January 31, 1966, pp. 1, 8).

The New York Times correspondent in Saigon saw the new campaign as signifying the end of the lull:

> Military developments this weekend laid to rest a feeling that the war in South Vietnam might be gradually 'fading away.' . . . Since November there had been few contacts with regular North Vietnamese troops and well-trained, 'main-force' Vietcong battalions. Some observers ascribed this to a withdrawal of Communist troops by Hanoi in an effort to slow military operations in response to the Johnson administration's diplomatic moves toward negotiations. Other observers, however, from the start ascribed the 'lull' to the fact that allied military units had had only bad luck and bad intelligence in mounting operations likely to make such contact (*NYT*, January 31, 1966, p. 1, 8).

On January 29, the day after contact was made, Washington sent a secret order to Pearl Harbor, which led to the resumption of bombings January 31. On that day both the President and the Secretary of State claimed that the continued "acts of violence in South Vietnam . . . made it clear" that the "negative attitudes of Hanoi and the Liberation Front" remained unchanged (*NYT*, February 1, 1966, p. 12). But the resumption must be seen as part of an escalation, coming as it did "at a time when military activity in general was being elevated by the United States" (*NYT*, January 31, 1966, p. 1).

Again, as on previous occasions, if there were military reasons for the timing of this "elevation," political ones also played a part. The United States still refused to contemplate negotiations with the NLF or Vietcong. Mr. Rusk put it unambiguously on January 28:

> If the Vietcong come to the conference table as full partners, they will be in a sense have been (sic) victorious in the very aims that South Vietnam and the United States are pledged to prevent (*NYT*, January 29, 1966, p. 2).

By this time, it was common knowledge that, as the Mansfield Report had declared, "dominance of the countryside rests largely in the hands of the Vietcong" (*NYT*, January 8, p. 2). Yet the objective of negotiations to end the war was still subordinated to the goal of denying and ending their *de facto* control of the countryside. Mr. Rusk, at least, still viewed United States policy as one of teaching Communism the lesson that "aggression" would not pay:

> We have not yet achieved a situation in which small as well as large countries can live securely in peace, safe from outside threat *or attack by subversion* or the infiltration of men in arms. That is why the situation in Southeast Asia is so very important (*NYT*, January 22, 1966, p. 2; emphasis added).

We have said that the fourteen points released by the State Department (see Appendix A) come very close to satisfying the four points of Hanoi, except with respect to point three: settlement of the internal affairs of South Vietnam by the South Vietnamese people "in accordance with" the NLF program.[2] This point had been Mr. Rusk's ground for

[2] The thirteenth point merely quotes from the President's speech of July 28, 1965: "13. The President has said, 'The Viet-

not immediately accepting the alleged offer reported by La Pira and Fanfani. It is important to recall that the 1960 NLF program called for abolition of the pro-American regime in Saigon, and its replacement, not by the NLF itself, but by "a government of national and democratic union . . . composed of representatives of all social classes, of all nationalities, of the various political parties, of all religions." Under this coalition government, South Vietnam would then "elect a new National Assembly through universal suffrage."[3] Apparently the United States hoped to avoid any recognition of the NLF by reversing the order of events, and holding unprecedented "free elections" under the existing authoritarian Saigon regime. Max Frankel wrote on December 31, 1965, from Washington that the third of the four points was

> the only really unacceptable condition for the Johnson Administration. Leading officials here see this as the real obstacle to a settlement. They are willing to meet the other points by promising—on the assumption that Hanoi would settle for the promise—an eventual American withdrawal, respect for the 1954 Geneva Accords, and eventual reunification of Vietnam by the Vietnamese themselves. But they want to leave behind a sovereign and independent South Vietnam with a government chosen by 'free elections,' which they contend would mean a non-Communist government (*NYT*, January 1, 1966, p. 3).

However, the NLF, which for a year now had controlled about half of the South Vietnamese population and perhaps three-quarters of the countryside, had insisted in its five points that negotiations recognize it as the "sole genuine representative of the South Vietnamese people," and grant them a "decisive voice." Since at least mid-April 1965, Hanoi too had repeatedly insisted on the NLF five points, as well as their own four points, as the basis for negotiations. Not to have done so would have been in effect for Hanoi to re-

---

cong would not have difficulty being represented and having their views represented if for a moment Hanoi decided she wanted to cease aggression. I don't think that would be an insurmountable problem.'"

[3] Program of the National Liberation Front of South Vietnam, in Raskin and Fall, *The Viet-Nam Reader*, p. 216.

pudiate the ambitions of the NLF for recognition—a politically impossible position. Viewed in this light, the fourteen points by themselves amounted, once again, to a "safely unacceptable offer."

On January 20, U Thant addressed himself implicitly to the questions of the NLF by suggesting

> that all elements of the South Vietnamese people, including presumably the Communist National Liberation Front, should be represented in the country's postwar government. Concrete proposals on this point at this time by the United States or any other party concerned might hasten the start of negotiations, Mr. Thant said. It would be difficult to justify a refusal to negotiate once such proposals were made, he remarked (*NYT*, January 21, 1966, p. 1).

The most authoritative confirmation that the major diplomatic issue was now recognition of the NLF was eventually supplied by no less a source than Ho Chi Minh. On January 28, 1966, one day before President Johnson ordered a resumption of bombing, Hanoi Radio broadcast a letter which Ho Chi Minh had sent on January 24 to the heads of other Communist-bloc countries, in which he analyzed the deficiencies of the fourteen points as part of the United States' "sham peace trick." (An almost identical letter was sent on this day to General de Gaulle, *LM*, February 1, 1966, p. 5). It is important to remember that President Johnson cited this letter as grounds for his decision to resume bombing, inasmuch as it contained "only denunciation and rejection":

> The answer of Hanoi to all is the answer that was published three days ago; they persist in aggression, they insist on the surrender of South Vietnam to Communism. It is therefore very plain that there is no readiness or willingness to talk (*NYT*, February 1, 1966, p. 12).

But Ho's letter contained more than "denunciation and rejection"; it spelled out what was wrong with the fourteen points from the North Vietnamese point of view, and what should be added to them:

> If the United States really wants peace, it must recognize the NFLSV (National Front for the Liberation of South Vietnam) as the sole genuine representative of the people of South Vietnam, and engage in negotiations with it. In accordance with the aspiration of the people of South Vietnam and the spirit of the 1954 Geneva Agreements on Vietnam, the NFLSV is fighting to achieve independence, democracy, peace, and neutrality in South Vietnam and to advance toward the peaceful reunification of the fatherland. If the United States really respects the right to self-determination of the people of South Vietnam, it cannot but approve this correct program of the National Front for Liberation (*NYT*, January 29, 1966, p. 2).[4]

The first of these sentences quotes from the language of the NLF five points ("sole genuine representative") but falls short of them, since nothing is said about granting the NLF a "decisive voice." But the last sentence is especially interesting for our purposes, since it might be interpreted as an answer to the objection raised by Mr. Rusk in the Fanfani-La Pira correspondence of the previous month—that respect for the Geneva Agreements of 1954 could in no way oblige the United States to recognize the *1960* program of the NLF.[5] The objectives of independence, democracy, peace, neutrality, and peaceful reunification are in fact all envisaged in the 1954 Agreements. These stipulations about the NLF were not at all (in our view) a "safely unacceptable offer," nor was the demand which followed:

> If the U.S. Government really wants a peaceful settlement, it must accept the four-point stand of the DRV Government and prove this by actual deeds. It must end unconditionally and for good all bombing raids and other war acts against the DRV. Only in this way can a political solution to the Vietnam problem be envisaged (*Ibid*).

It is of course true that the same letter was filled with

[4] Secretary Rusk, in justifying the resumption of bombings, cited only the first of these sentences, as constituting an "unmistakable" clarification of Hanoi's "negative attitude" (*NYT*, February 1, 1966, p. 12).

[5] If this were a correct interpretation, it would imply that the question of whether a new government should precede or follow elections could be settled at the Conference itself.

angry invective against the United States, on the grounds that an offer to negotiate in the context of new escalations was in effect no offer:

> In his 12 January 1966 message read before the U.S. Congress, President Johnson (explained) that it was the policy of the United States not to pull out of South Vietnam. . . . At the very moment when the U.S. Government (puts) forward the so-called new peace effort, it is frantically increasing U.S. strength in South Vietnam. It is stepping up the terrorist raids, resorting to the scorched-earth policy. . . .

These charges may have amounted to "denunciation," as President Johnson claimed, but they were unfortunately true.

We do not believe that a reading of Ho Chi Minh's letter will bear out President Johnson's charge that in it the North Vietnamese "insist on the surrender of South Vietnam to Communism." We find an even greater departure from candor in Secretary Rusk's claim that

> they (the DRV and NLF) made clear their negative view by deeds as well as words throughout the period of the suspension of bombing. Infiltration of men and material from the North into South Vietnam continued at a high level. Acts of violence in South Vietnam itself continued with relatively minor fluctuations, at virtually the same high record set in the last quarter of 1965. By these acts they made it clear that their purpose remained what it has been from the beginning, namely to take over South Vietnam by force (*NYT*, February 1, 1966, p. 12).

The "high level" of infiltration was variously estimated in this period to run from about 1,700 to about 4,500 men a month, or from less than one percent to about two percent of the total estimated Communist forces in South Vietnam. Between January 18-28 alone, the United States admitted introducing some 6,000 men (*NYT*, January 29, 1966, p. 3); the U.S. increase during the 37 days of the pause was apparently more than 14,000, the total number of DRV troops alleged by the Mansfield Report to be present in South Vietnam. "Acts of violence" had been increasing throughout 1965 to a new high of 1,133 in the last week of 1965; yet the limited available evidence suggests a distinct falling off hereafter:

Week Ending:	No. of Incidents:	Source:
Dec. 4, 1965	1,038 (a new high)	*NYT*, Jan. 6, 1966, p. 3
Dec. 25, 1965 (Christmas truce)	861	*NYT*, Jan. 6, 1966, p. 3
Jan. 1, 1966 (first week of pause)	1,133 (a new high)	*NYT*, Jan. 6, 1966, p. 3
Jan. 8, 1966	973	*NYT*, Jan. 13, 1966, p. 3
Jan. 15, 1966	807	*NYT*, Jan. 20, 1966, p. 3
Jan. 22, 1966 (Truce of Tet)	Statistics not reported: casualty figures only given.	*NYT*, Jan. 27, 1966, p. 3
Jan. 29, 1966 (Truce of Tet)	Statistics not reported: casualty figures only given.	*NYT*, Feb. 3, 1966, p. 1

But Mr. Rusk's decision to talk of "acts of violence" committed by guerillas obscured the virtual withdrawal from combat of organized NLF and DRV forces; and his reply to a question on this point carried the obfuscation still further:

> Q. Mr. Secretary, how do you interpret the fact that there's been no large-scale direct contact with North Vietnamese troops since the latter part of November?
> A. Well, there's some ambiguity about that. There seems to have been some contact sometime in December and there are indications at the present time that there is very active contact with North Vietnamese forces there. We've not seen anything on the ground from which one could draw political conclusions indicating that Hanoi was prepared to pull away or hold its hand or move toward peace in this situation (*NYT*, February 1, 1966, p. 12).[6]

This "very active contact with North Vietnamese forces" had

[6] Mr. Rusk's testimony on January 21 is also intriguing. At that time, in the middle of the lull, he said: "We have been listen-

taken place at Anthai in Binhdinh Province in Central Vietnam (*NYT*, January 31, 1966, p. 1), and had only been reported after the launching by the United States of "a general (amphibious) offensive in that area" (*Ibid*). Inasmuch as the contact with North Vietnamese regulars took place "in a sandy landing zone" (p. 8), it is clear that the offensive operation was American rather than North Vietnamese. From one to two months' lull in the fighting, followed by an unexplained U.S. offensive, somehow had "made it clear" to Secretary Rusk that North Vietnam's aggressive intentions remained unchanged.

What is the real explanation for the decision to resume bombing North Vietnam? John Pomfret reported to *The New York Times* from Washington that

> The President, according to informed sources, never was too keen on the pause, to begin with. However, he saw it as an opportunity to persuade foreign capitals and public opinion at home that he was serious about the search for a peaceful solution to the conflict in Vietnam (*NYT*, February 1, 1966, p. 13).

The President had originally decided on the pause after a poll had shown that seventy-three percent of the American people favored one (*NYT*, January 28, 1966, p. 12). The public-relations aspect of the pause was perhaps strongest at its beginning, during the so-called "peace missions" (one of which, that of the Vice-President, actually involved the search for additional troops from the Philippines and Korea). Nevertheless, the pause in the bombing was gradually acquiring political significance, in the context of both a *de facto* lull in the fighting, and the gradual definition of the question of

---

ing for sounds other than the sounds of bombs and grenades and mortars in South Vietnam. I regret that I cannot report to you any positive and encouraging response to the hopes of the overwhelming majority of mankind" (*NYT*, January 22, 1966, p. 2). Apparently (this part of the testimony was not reprinted) the Secretary "attached little significance to the reports of some decline in the number of military engagements in South Vietnam. On the contrary, he said that the indications were that the Communists would intensify their activity after the Lunar New Year holiday" (*NYT*, January 22, 1966, p. 1). By holding its hand, the United States could have allowed time to prove Mr. Rusk's hypothesis. Instead it chose to end its truce six hours ahead of the time announced by the NLF.

recognizing the NLF as the main issue which still prevented negotiations.

In retrospect, it appears that the North Vietnamese had given precisely the kinds of sign that the United States had reportedly asked for in its communication of December 29. According to *The New York Times,*

> the sort of sign the United States is looking for could be either an oral proposal of negotiations that would eliminate, or at least tone down, some of the North Vietnamese demands found unacceptable in the past or some tangible sign of a decrease in military activity or infiltration from the north. Perhaps the most difficult of North Vietnam's demands has been its insistence that the Vietcong participate in any postwar South Vietnamese government, and that the program of the new government be modeled on the program of the Communist-led National Liberation Front (*NYT*, December 29, 1965, p. 2).

The decrease in military activity had been noticeable; the allusions to the 1960 NLF program had been refined away. What remained was Hanoi's insistence that the NLF itself be recognized as representative. That this was the issue may have been known to U Thant on January 20, when he appealed to the United States to concede it. It was almost certainly known to Mr. Rusk on January 21, when he rejected this possibility, for at his press conference of that day he implied (by his own repeated efforts to evade a clear answer) that there had already been a secret response from the Communist side, albeit "nothing that Washington found 'positive or encouraging,'" (*NYT*, January 22, 1966, p. 1).[7]

Once the United States had decided not to recognize the NLF or accept its participation in a government or conference, the pause in the bombing could only be regarded as an embarrassing liability which must somehow be terminated. Indeed, the threat again existed of unwelcome negotiations, inasmuch as pressures for peace were building up (through the encouragement of the pause and the lull) which might soon get out of control. For the first time, the political processes of the American nation were beginning to reflect a

[7] The transcript of Mr. Rusk's repeated evasive answers ("we have not received the kind of response for which we were hoping") will be found in *I. F. Stone's Weekly*, January 31, 1966, p. 4.

serious division of opinion about the wisdom of the war. More and more people within the country, as well as outside, were now calling for recognition of the NLF. In rejecting this on January 21, Mr. Rusk had claimed to represent the wishes of the "overwhelming majority" of the South Vietnamese people; but it was becoming less and less clear that he represented the wishes of the American people. A still greater pressure was building up, both at home and abroad, to continue the pause:

> The Administration is under considerable pressure from abroad to prolong the pause in the bombing of North Vietnam well beyond the holiday cease-fire now going into effect. The Governments of Britain, France, and Japan, all allies of the United States, and the Communist Governments of Europe as well as the governments of a number of nonaligned nations are said to be pleading for several more weeks or even months of restraint (*NYT*, January 20, 1966, p. 1).

> The gap between what the United States is doing and what most of the United Nations thinks should be done is growing wider every day. If the Johnson Administration resumes the bombing of North Vietnam, the outcry here is expected to be more shrill than at any time in the past (*NYT*, January 28, 1966, p. 1).

Significant elements of Congress were also becoming restive at the prospect of renewed bombings and possibly of expanded war. On January 24, the President spoke to a bipartisan group of twenty Congressional leaders, some of whom

> left with the impression that Mr. Johnson was moving toward a decision to resume the bombing. The next day, a group of Senators began trying to organize colleagues in both parties to oppose resumption of the air strikes against North Vietnam (*NYT*, February 1, 1966, p. 13).

An AP survey of the Senate in this period found only twenty-five senators willing to say they favored resumption of bombing, while an equal number opposed it (*Washington Star*, January 26, 1966). Senator Fulbright requested in vain that the Senate Foreign Relations Committee be consulted before resumption of bombing (*NYT*, January 26, 1966, p. 1). But the press began to speculate that an end to the lull was near. Then on January 28, for the first time, Senator Fulbright and other members of the Senate Foreign Relations Committee "openly challenged . . . the legality of the nation's deepening military involvement in the Vietnam war and demanded a detailed explanation of Administration policy" (*NYT*, January 29, 1966, p. 1). This unprecedented revolt in the U.S. Senate was followed, one day later, by the order to resume bombing. We see that, once again, the United States had decided on a military escalation in the face of pressures which threatened to lead to a political settlement. The only novelty in the period of January 1966 is that, for the first time, a major "threat" of pacification was coming from inside the United States itself.

Epilogue:

The Buddhist-Led Opposition Movement and the Bombing of Hanoi and Haiphong (February—July 1966)

AUTHORS' NOTE

AUGUST 2, 1966

The commentator who attempts to deal with such rapidly changing events as the war in Vietnam will always remain at least one step behind. The original Citizens' White Paper, which covered nine periods of the Vietnamese conflict through January of 1966, was printed privately in the late spring. In the course of the months which elapsed between the completion of the final draft and its release to the press on June 26, important and dramatic developments have occurred in South Vietnam. The disaffection with the Saigon regime among the non-Communist population of South Vietnam, which we attempted to document for an earlier period, had taken on new and important dimensions. The people of South Vietnam had found themselves involved in a civil war within a civil war, with government forces emerging as the momentary victor over the people they purported to represent; and as the internal conflict progressed, U. S. planes began to intensify the bombing of the North. Since these events seem to confirm in many ways some of the points we had made in the original White Paper, we regretted the fact that our document had been completed too early for their inclusion.

Then, on June 29—only three days after our document was released—came the bombing of the oil depots of Hanoi and Haiphong, bringing the escalation of the war into what can only be described as a new (and still more dangerous) phase.

We now have the opportunity to look back at these tragic events and subject them to the same type of analysis which we have attempted to give to the preceding nine periods; that is, we shall try to uncover the "politics of escalation" for the period of February-July 1966. Yet even as we are writing, events are outstripping us. On this very day, August 2, 1966, word has been received that American bombs have once again been dropped within the city limits of Haiphong, in close proximity to Soviet merchant ships. Only three days earlier, on July 30, American bombers for the first time pummeled the demilitarized zone separating the two Vietnams. Now there is talk of a new phase in the escalation that would involve the mining of Haiphong harbor (despite the presence of Soviet shipping), the destruction of the Red River dikes (despite the death of tens of thousands of civilians that this would entail), or even the invasion of North Vietnam. We can only hope that these calls for still further expansion of warfare will not have become evident by the time this volume reaches the bookstores, and that, instead, steps will have been taken to lead America out of the political and military quagmire of Vietnam.

SUMMARY: The period of February-July 1966 may best be understood by focusing attention on the basic elements of the Vietnamese situation with which the reader is by now familiar: the internal political situation in South Vietnam, the course of military escalation, and diplomatic peace overtures.

The internal political situation was characterized by dramatic attempts on the part of Buddhists, students, and other indigenous elements, including an important segment of Vietnamese Catholics, to wrest control of the Saigon government from the hands of the military junta, headed by General Ky. As we already know, Buddhist-student opposition to previous Saigon regimes had been widespread in the past, so that the antigovernment movement that began in the early spring of 1966 came as no surprise. The breadth of the new antijunta coalition, however, and the perseverance of its partisans were both unprecedented. So, too, were the openness of the demonstrators' neutralism, the explicitness of their desire for a compromise settlement with the NLF, and the strength of their opposition to U.S. policy in their country. More than ever before, the U.S. government was faced with the threat that a broadly based civilian government might come to power in Saigon, negotiate a settlement with the NLF, and demand the partial or complete withdrawal of American troops from Vietnam.

Spokesmen for the Washington Administration made little effort to conceal the fact that they viewed such developments as a threat. Nor did the logistic and financial support provided by the American command for General Ky's efforts against the dissenters convince many people that our government was neutral in this internal Vietnamese struggle. In late May, when Ky finally succeeded in breaking the back (for the moment, at least) of the opposition movement, American officials greeted the news with an uninhibited sigh of relief and pointed to the scheduling of "free" elections (from which not only Communists but neutralists were to be excluded) as vindication of their position.

Turning to the question of military escalation, there is evidence that once again the Administration, by resorting to dramatic new bombings, was saved from the imminent possibility of unwelcome negotiations or compromise. As with regard to previous periods, we do not offer this analysis as a comprehensive explanation of American escalation of the war against the North. Pressure from so-called "hawks" (civilian as well as military) in favor of greater escalation has existed independently of political turmoil in Saigon, Danang, and Hué, while "doves" have found themselves in the defensive position of attempting to restrict military operations to their present, already devastating, level. The record seems to indicate, however, that during the spring of 1966, the timing of specific acts of escalation—the decision to proceed with a not-yet implemented bombing plan, for example—was correlated with the internal difficulties of the Ky regime. If offensive operations against Viet-

cong forces in the South had to be scaled down because of the distracting influence of antigovernment demonstrations, American commitment to its (and General Ky's) hard-line in Vietnam could nevertheless be expressed by new escalations in the North, and the General's faltering prestige could once again be upheld. Thus the bombing of North Vietnam was intensified in late March and early April just as the antigovernment movement in the South was gaining momentum. Even more significantly, the greatest blows to Ky's prestige in the period under discussion, the withdrawal of his troops from Danang on April 5 in the face of adamant opposition from the population of that city and the consequent strengthening of the antigovernment movement, was followed on April 12 by a qualitatively significant escalation of the bombing of the North (as had been predicted in Le Monde on April 8.) Further intensification of the bombing continued over the next few weeks, as Ky was gradually able to divide and conquer the opposition movement (Danang capitulated on May 24).

The third element of our analysis, the influence of international peace moves on the diplomatic front on the timing of escalation, may also be demonstrated with regard to this period. As has been mentioned earlier, the experience of two and a half years of the escalation-negotiation syndrome had soured Hanoi to the prospects of a negotiated settlement, and the position of the North Vietnamese had hardened somewhat by the beginning of the new year. This remained the case for most of the period now under discussion and, combined with the increasing American commitment, left little doubt in the minds of those who had pressed for peace talks in the past —de Gaulle, U Thant, and others—that initiatives at this juncture would be a wasted effort. Thus the "threat" of international initiatives for negotiations barely existed in the spring of 1966.

Some time in the middle of June, not long after the anti-Ky demonstrations in South Vietnam had subsided, this situation suddenly changed. The change took the form of an apparent softening in the attitude of Hanoi (reported by Agence France Presse on June 15). It was quickly followed by signs that the international wheels were again in motion. Within a week's time, the secret Ronning mission had visited Hanoi and returned to Canada, U Thant had returned to the diplomatic front with some interesting new proposals, and a French mission headed by Jean Sainteny was preparing to visit Peking and the North Vietnamese capital. Whether these new efforts by third parties were precipitated by awareness of a change of posture in Hanoi or by reports of American preparations for a new and dangerous escalation of the war is impossible to say, although by now it should be clear that the two hypotheses are not contradictory. Be that as it may, it is an indisputable fact that news of the Administration's impending decision to bomb oil depots within the city limits of Hanoi and Haiphong began to leak to the public precisely as the démarches of the French, the Canadians, and the Secretary-General began to get underway. President Johnson's tough speech of July 18, widely interpreted as a prelude to escalation, was made either while Ronning was still in Hanoi or shortly after his departure; the now-famous newspaper leaks to the effect that the bombings were forthcoming began to appear only a few days after U Thant's ill-fated proposals of June 20; and the Sainteny mission was apparently unable to enter Hanoi on June 29 because the bombing was in progress. To this it should be added that although very little is known about the outcome of the Ronning mission, the Administration's claim that it was unsuccessful is contradicted by some evidence. There is reason to believe that the Canadians still considered their discussions with Hanoi to be in progress when the bombing began.

1. The Buddhist-Led Opposition Movement

The most dramatic event in South Vietnam during the period from February to July 1966 centered around the efforts of the Buddhist-led opposition to force Premier Nguyen Cao Ky to agree to free elections and to the formation of a civilian government. Overt Buddhist opposition, which had subsided in February 1965, burst out again when Premier Ky decided to move against his archrival General Nguyen Chanh Thi, commander of the I Corps area based on Danang. On March 10, 1966, Ky dismissed Thi. On March 14, a general strike broke out in Danang. The demonstration spread rapidly to Hué and Da Lat and finally to Saigon. By the second week after the ouster of Thi, anti-Americanism had become an important factor in the movement. Most of the soldiers of the I Corps supported the rebellion, as did the Mayor of Danang. On March 31, the first big demonstration broke out in Saigon, where crowds called for the execution of Ky and the chief of state Nguyen Van Thieu. Many Catholics joined the Buddhists in demanding the formation of a civilian government (*Le Monde,* March 31, April 1, 1966). On April 2, military leaders met in Saigon and decided to take action against the rebels. On April 4, several South Vietnamese battalions were transported to Danang in American planes but remained on the American air base. On April 5, Ky flew to Danang but decided not to move into the city. Ky's show of weakness at Danang brought about an intensification of popular demonstrations in South Vietnam's major cities, with fears arising in Washington that the Ky regime would fall, and be succeeded by a new government less favorable to the United States presence. (For an account of the events between March 10 and April 5, see Robert Shaplen, "Letter From Saigon," *New Yorker,* April 16, 1966, pp. 155-168).[1]

On April 7, Max Frankel reported from Washington that "The Johnson Administration's overriding concern in South Vietnam's political crisis is said to be the survival of the ten-man military junta with or without Premier Nguyen Cao Ky at its head" (*NYT,* April 7, 1966). The thinking behind the Administration's commitment to the junta was indicated

[1] The situation in the first days of April was so serious that William D. Moyers, Presidential Press Secretary, cancelled his projected visit to South Vietnam. However, on April 2, Cyrus Vance, Deputy Defense Secretary, arrived in Saigon. *Agence France Presse* commented that "this visit foreshadows an announcement by Washington of the sending of substantial numbers of new troops. . . . Similarly, the Americans intend to intensify their bombings of the South." (*Le Monde,* April 3-4, 1966).

in an article by Chalmers M. Roberts from Washington: "If Saigon's military leaders grant the kind of political change the Buddhists are demanding, it could mean a coalition regime in the South able and willing to negotiate with the North to end the Vietnamese war." Roberts added: "Officials here are mute on the prospect but privately are well aware of the possibility. So far, they do not look upon it with favor, however much Washington would like to find a way to end the war" (*San Francisco Chronicle*, April 12, 1966).[2]

The increasing demands for an end to the war voiced by the demonstrators, coupled with rising anti-Americanism, left little doubt that if the Buddhist movement had succeeded, attempts at negotiations would have been undertaken. The Buddhist priest Nhat Hanh, who toured the United States and Western Europe in May, spoke of the horrible devastation visited upon his country and the desire of the Buddhists to set up a government they saw as the only viable popular force able to deal with the National Liberation Front.[3] The leader of the French section of Vietnamese Overseas Buddhists, Le Kim Chi, stated openly that the Buddhists were seeking a negotiated peace with the NLF (*Le Monde*, May 31, 1966). Shortly after Ky's retreat at Danang, however, when a reporter from *Paris Match* asked Secretary Rusk whether the United States would leave South Vietnam if asked to do so by a new civilian government, Rusk responded evasively:

> "That is a very hypothetical question, because I do not envisage the eventualities of which you speak. The commitments undertaken by the United States according to the terms of treaties derive from requests for assistance from South Vietnam. If this situation should change, a new situation would come into being. Since I

[2] See also Tom Wicker's column "Dilemma in Viet Nam," *NYT*, April 1, 1966, and Shaplen, *loc. cit.*, p. 168.

[3] In his article "The Real Revolution in South Vietnam" (which, in the spring of 1966, became a matter of controversy in the United States), George A. Carver, Jr. said that ". . . only the Buddhists now seem to have any effective mass organization" (*Foreign Affairs*, April, 1965, p. 402). The "real revolution" that Carver talked about appeared to be coming into being at this time, except that its nationalism was being directed against the United States.

do not expect that to happen, I would rather not engage in speculation" (quoted in *Le Monde*, April 14, 1966.)

Ky's retreat at Danang was followed by a sharp deterioration of the political situation. Demonstration followed demonstration in Saigon. The northern provinces slipped out of the government's control. For the first time since the anti-Diem movement, Buddhist monks and nuns engaged in self-immolation. As police and paratroopers moved against the demonstrators, thousands of citizens placed Buddhist altars in the streets to block their way. Ky gave in to the pressure and promised elections for August 15. However, it soon became clear that Ky had no intention of stepping down. Early in May he announced that the election deadline would have to be postponed until October. Then he indicated that the military government would remain in power for at least another year. The events of early May, however, made it clear that Ky's real aim was to break the Buddhist resistance. On May 16, the Buddhists completely occupied Danang and appealed to the United States to intervene against Ky (*San Francisco Examiner*, May 16, 1966). The following day, Ky sent troops to Danang. This time they entered the city and surrounded the rebel-held pagodas. Danang surrendered on May 24. However, the issue had already been decided on May 17, when the Buddhists were unable to muster sufficient counterforce against Ky's troops. It was only a matter of time before the beleaguered pagodas had to surrender. The fall of Hué a short time later was anticlimactic.

2. The Pattern of Escalation

It is important to remember that both in Washington and in Saigon there was continuing pressure to escalate the war in the North as well as in the South. Thus, only a few days after the resumption of the bombing of North Vietnam on January 31, Reuben Salazar of the Times-Post Service reported from Saigon that "American military officials—on a strictly unofficial basis—are conducting a campaign here to intensify the war effort against North Vietnam" (*San Francisco Chronicle*, February 4, 1966). Given the past record, there can be little doubt that the American military in South

Vietnam has consistently advocated a strong "hawk" policy in regard to the war. However, these pressures were not confined to the American military in South Vietnam. On March 22, James Reston reported that "the pressure seems to be building up in the Senate for a policy of bombing, mining or blockading the North Vietnamese harbor of Haiphong" (*NYT*, March 23, 1966). One of the leading proponents of escalation was Senator Richard Russell of Georgia. Russell had advocated the bombing of Haiphong at least as early as December 1965. Now Reston quoted him as saying:

> "I do not think we can afford to let this war drift on and on as it is now. . . . Search and destroy tactics may, after ten or twelve years, bring the Vietcong to their knees, but the American people are going to be very unhappy about it, and someone who comes along and says: 'I will go in and clean this thing up in six months,' will, I'm afraid, have some advantage over the Senators who say: 'Let's play this thing along for ten or twelve years as we're going now."

In addition to these "hawk" pressures, there were others coming from Ambassador Lodge and from the Joint Chiefs of Staff. On May 20, Robert S. Allen and Paul Scott reported that "Ambassador Henry Cabot Lodge strongly favors bombing the huge oil depot near the port of Haiphong." They added: "The Joint Chiefs of Staff have repeatedly recommended destruction of this crucial Communist supply center" (*Oakland Tribune*, May 20, 1966). We might compare Senator Russell's logic that escalation to the north is the only alternative to fighting a protracted war in the South with that expressed by Premier Ky late in July, when he suggested an invasion of North Vietnam and a confrontation with China as an alternative to a long war in South Vietnam (*NYT*, July 26, 1966).

Since the "hawk" pressure for continuing escalation appears to have been constant, the question of the *timing* of the various escalation steps arises. James Reston has argued that "everything in the Johnson strategy seems to be done in twos—something for the hawks and something for the doves" (*NYT*, February 9, 1966). Arthur Krock, also writing from Washington, had this to say about the timing factor in the President's decision-making:

> The administration long rejected proposals that the offices of the United Nations be enlisted in bringing about a cease-fire in Vietnam. But when it reversed its position, the Administration simultaneously resumed the bombing of North Vietnam. . . .
> A statement by Secretary of State Dean Rusk before the House Committee on Foreign Affairs prophesying and encouraging eventual friendly relations with Communist China was released for publication last Saturday. . . . The day after this release, United States aircraft bombed the environs of Hanoi for the first time. This bombing, calculated to intensify the hostility of the present government in Peking, requires days of preparation. What is the explanation of the timing of the Rusk release and the action certain to defer any possible attainment of its objective? (*NYT*, April 19, 1966).[4]

As James Reston, commenting on this phenomenon, asked, "Do these policies complement one another or cancel each other out?"

Since, in retrospect, the "hawks" have been getting pretty much what they demand, what Arthur Krock called the "timing" of these various actions takes on considerable importance.

To understand the timing factor, let us look at the overall picture of American military actions during the period of the South Vietnamese political crisis. On April 20, testifying before the Senate Foreign Relations Committee, Secretary McNamara gave an indication of the intensity of the American war effort in Vietnam. He noted that, in March, the Air Force had flown 4,700 sorties or twenty-five per cent more than planned. However, "in the first days of April, the number of missions flown against communications lines in Vietnam exceeded those for all of March." The appalling destruction wreaked is suggested by the fact that in March, American planes dropped 50,000 tons of bombs over Vietnam, compared to an average of 48,000 tons dropped monthly over Europe and Africa in World War II (*NYT*, April 21, 1966).

The Secretary's testimony implied a greatly stepped up

[4] Rusk's statement on China came on April 17. One day later, American planes struck two missile sites less than twenty miles from Hanoi, the closest they had come to the capital up to that time (*NYT*, April 17, 18, 1966).

air effort during the latter part of March and the early part of April, coinciding with the period of the South Vietnamese political crisis. However, from his further comments it would appear that the intensification took place largely over *North* Vietnam. McNamara admitted that "missions against other targets are running lower than in March . . . because of 'political disorders' and the lower level of fighting generally" (*Ibid.*). Assistant Secretary of Defense Arthur Sylvester admitted the same when he said that "there has been a temporary reduction in sorties within South Vietnam." He added that "one reason is that the Army of the Republic of South Vietnam is mounting fewer attacks requiring U.S. air support" (*San Francisco Chronicle,* April 12, 1966). Not only were South Vietnamese troops "mounting fewer attacks" in many parts of the country (and especially in the rebellious northern provinces), but a dock strike in Danang forced the use of American soldiers to unload the ships. Both South Vietnamese troops and civilians rejected American appeals to help unload the vessels (*NYT,* April 12, 1966).

Since the disinclination of the South Vietnamese Army (ARVN) to go out and fight has been repeatedly noted in the past, the further decline in ARVN actions must have indeed been remarkable. In addition to their disinclination to fight, the desertion rate remained high. On June 28, 1966, the *New York Post* reported from Saigon that "the South Vietnam Army's desertion rate continues to be a scandal—by American standards at least." In 1965, 113,000 troops had deserted. In the first six months of 1966, 67,000 deserted—an increase of almost 20 percent.

Of equally great significance is the fact that the Vietcong slowed down their military activity during the crisis. During the first week of April, Vietcong military activity slowed down to the lowest level in 16 months in South Vietnam's forty-five provinces. Communist-originated actions went below 100, compared to a monthly average of 175. Yet, while combat between the two Vietnamese sides had dropped sharply, "United States Marines in the I Corps area have continued active pursuit of the enemy since the outbreak of antigovernment demonstrations in the north." The first (of three) hypotheses offered by American officials for the decline in Vietcong-initiated actions was that the Vietcong feared that actions on their part might force the pro- and antigovernment forces back together (*NYT,* April 12, 1966).

If we piece these diverse fragments of information together, a pattern emerges. When the crisis broke out on March 10, the ARVN forces gradually disengaged from such combat as they had still been engaged in. The Vietcong declined to go on the attack, to the "surprise" of the Americans (*Ibid.*). In view of the NLF declarations in the past that they would be willing to negotiate with a Saigon regime, one can surmise that the NLF reduced its war effort in the hope that a new government might come to power in Saigon with which it could negotiate.[5]

Thus it would appear that as the political crisis worsened in South Vietnam and the South Vietnamese army withdrew from combat, and as the Vietcong, hoping to assist neutralist movement, relaxed its pressure, the United States intensified its air actions against North Vietnam in late March and early April.

So far, we have noted a quantitative increase in American escalation during the period of crisis. However, only days after Ky's retreat at Danang on April 5, the United States made a major qualitative change in the air war.[6] On April 12, the United States, for the first time in the war, sent B-52 bombers over North Vietnam (to bomb the Mu Ghi Pass south of Vinh). This "stirred speculation that a pattern of saturation B-52 bombing might be in the works to supplement tactical air attacks on the North" (*San Francisco Chronicle,* April 12, 1966). As if to drive the point home that there had been a qualitative change in the escalation pattern, James Reston reported on April 27 that "the official policy of the United States is that our bombers are now free to attack the base of any planes that intercept our

[5] That Hanoi envisaged the possibility of negotiating with a new government in Saigon was reported by Takashi Oka, *Christian Science Monitor* correspondent in Saigon, as early as March 9, 1966. Oka also reported that Communist (notably Polish) and Western-bloc diplomats were exploring the possibility of reconstituting the Saigon government.

[6] *Le Monde,* on April 8, predicted a new escalation: "The Americans, aware of the reverses which the present demonstrations represent for them, are getting ready to intensify their air raids north of the 17th parallel. The question, moreover, is to render the port of Haiphong unusable." The French paper quoted a *New York Times* Washington correspondent as saying that the aim of the bombings would be "to try to reestablish the equilibrium broken to [the Americans'] disadvantage by the disorders in central Vietnam."

fliers in North Vietnam, even if those bases are inside Communist China" (*San Francisco Chronicle,* April 27, 1966). Ironically, on the same day, Tom Wicker reported from Washington that "President Johnson is planning no major policy shifts or new initiatives as a result of the recent political unrest in South Vietnam and a new upsurge of criticism in this country." That the new "official policy" of no sanctuary was not mere words was shown by the shooting down of a Chinese plane over Chinese territory.

Thus we return again to the question of timing. The B-52 raids were launched just a week after Ky's retreat at Danang. This would suggest that—as had happened in the past—they were designed, in part at least, to bolster Ky's morale, or more correctly, that of the military junta to the survival of which the United States was committed. Washington thus showed its determination to continue with the war. We might also note that there were some significant intensifications of the air war over North Vietnam early in May. On May 8, American planes bombed a vital bridge linking North Vietnam with China. On the following day, all four rail links with Hanoi were cut. On May 14, three days before Ky's move against Danang, *Le Monde* reported from Washington that for the first time official circles were openly threatening to attack the air bases around Hanoi. These intensifications took place precisely at the time that the Rumanian mission headed by Emil Bodnaras was in Hanoi, presumably sounding out the North Vietnamese about the possibilities of peace negotiations.

Exactly how Ky was able to achieve his victory over the Buddhists remains unclear. It is certainly possible that behind the scenes American pressure was applied to strengthen Ky and weaken the opposition forces. At the crucial moment of the second confrontation in Danang, soldiers of I Corps were generally absent and Ky's men were able to take the pagodas. After Nguyen Chanh Thi had rebelled in March, Ky had sent, successively, two trusted lieutenants to take command of I Corps. Both of them went over to the rebellion. It is therefore hard to believe that the rebel soldiers spontaneously rediscovered their loyalty to Ky. Perhaps someday we shall find out the details of the story.

However, the escalation pattern had the effect of making it clear to the South Vietnamese, to the North Vietnamese, and to all, that the Johnson Administration would not tolerate any move to end the war through negotiations among the Vietnamese themselves.

Once the political crisis had eased, the pace of the war could again be stepped up by American military forces in the South, and a series of ground actions launched against the Vietcong. On June 10, *The New York Times* revealed American plans to send an additional 100,000 troops to South Vietnam to start a big offensive to open up Route 1 between Saigon and Hué. On June 2, the U.S. Air Force carried out the most massive raid of the war (against Yen Bai, about 100 miles northwest of Hanoi on the strategic railroad going to China). However, the next qualitative change in the escalation is best seen in the context of the larger international situation.

3. International Moves Toward Negotiations

The resumption of bombing on January 31, 1966, had dashed international hopes for a negotiated settlement. The United Nations quickly receded as a possible forum for arranging a settlement of the Vietnamese conflict (if it ever was one), and all sides evinced negative attitudes toward negotiations. However, statements kept on coming from Washington that President Johnson was "as anxious as ever for a negotiated settlement, but his view is that the Vietcong and their North Vietnamese supporters are convinced that they can win the war militarily and take over South Vietnam" (*San Francisco Chronicle,* April 27, 1966). That there was some truth to this assessment is indicated in an *Agence France Presse* dispatch from Hanoi on June 3 (*Le Monde,* June 3, 1966). *Agence France Presse* reported a "hardening" of the North Vietnamese attitude and a confidence that the situation of the Vietcong, just before the beginning of the monsoon season, was "favorable." In anticipation of a worsening of the air raids, one half of the 1,200,000 population of Hanoi had evacuated. However, *Agence France Presse* also reported that "at the same time [foreign observers in Hanoi] believed more than ever in the determination of the North

Vietnamese leaders to avoid an extension of the conflict," meaning a further "internationalization" of the war.

During this six-month period, China's attitude, at least in public, remained uncompromising, although the Chinese became very preoccupied with their internal purge, which erupted violently early in May. Reports on the purge virtually displaced news from Vietnam in the Chinese press. The Soviet attitude also hardened appreciably. During the Soviet Twenty-Third Party Congress, which was attended by North Vietnamese and NLF delegations (but not by the Chinese), strong support for the Vietnamese cause was voiced by all delegates. A cooling in the relationship between Peking and Hanoi did appear to have set in after the Congress, perhaps in connection with the Sino-Soviet feud over the transport of military equipment overland through China (a matter openly mentioned by Marshal Rodion Malinovsky, and for which he was publicly criticized by the Chinese; *Le Monde*, May 5, 1966). Nevertheless, it was reported that Russia and China finally reached agreement for the unobstructed transport of Soviet war material over Chinese territory (*Le Monde*, May 4, 1966).

Outside the Communist world, two leading international figures, Charles de Gaulle and U Thant, openly indicated that the prospects for peace negotiations in the immediate future were remote. In their meetings early in May, both agreed on this point (*Le Monde*, May 3, 1966). A week later, U Thant reiterated his pessimism. A Rumanian mission, headed by Deputy Premier Emil Bodnăras, which visited Moscow, Peking, and Hanoi early in May, was at first coolly received in Hanoi, but their reception warmed as the Rumanians apparently indicated stronger support for the North Vietnamese position. Peking reported little on the Rumanian mission, preferring to give more publicity to a visiting Albanian delegation. The inference seems plausible that Hanoi's position remained hard. However, as already noted, the Bodnaras mission coincided with a major series of American attacks on the perimeters of Hanoi, a factor which might have made the Rumanians more sympathetic to the North Vietnamese position.

Hanoi's attitude still appeared hard in early June. On June 15, however, *Agence France Presse* reported from Hanoi that "the idea of a peaceful solution to the conflict seems to be ripening in Hanoi." Foreign diplomatic observers in Hanoi "are struck by the change of atmosphere in the North

Vietnamese capital." *Agence France Presse* noted that Hanoi felt that its position was good, and that all countries, save China, wanted the war to end. However, *Agence France Presse* indicated, things had to go slowly, and Hanoi could not move right away (*Le Monde,* June 15, 1966). As far as China was concerned, though the rhetoric about continuing the fight went on, statements were made in Peking implying that the North Vietnamese would have to go on fighting alone and should not count on Chinese aid. Taken in conjunction with persisting Chinese accusations of Soviet collusion with the U.S. to bring about peace talks in Vietnam, it does not seem unreasonable to assume that Hanoi was beginning to look more favorably on negotiations, particularly when its hopes for a new government in Saigon had been dashed.

There appears to have been substance to this *Agence France Presse* report, for two important Western missions were soon dispatched to Hanoi: a Canadian mission led by the veteran Far Eastern expert Chester Ronning and a French mission led by another Far Eastern expert Jean Sainteny. As far as we can tell, nothing leaked out about Ronning's mission until he returned to Ottawa. On June 20, he reported to Canadian Foreign Minister Paul Martin, and the following day Martin stated that Canada was making some preliminary soundings to determine the bases for a settlement of the Vietnam conflict (*Le Monde,* June 23, 1966). Since the mission was secret, one might presume that Foreign Minister Martin would not have made any public statement if the results had been entirely negative. However, the same day (June 21), Assistant Secretary of State for Far Eastern Affairs, William P. Bundy, made a quick trip to Ottawa. Upon his return, the State Department issued a brief comment (reported in an equally brief and obscure item in *The New York Times,* June 23) that "no change had taken place in Hanoi's position." Yet, Bernard Fall reported later that:

> Just two weeks earlier, both French and Rumanian diplomats had been informed separately by high-ranking Chinese officials that, while Peking did not particularly relish the idea of negotiations between Hanoi and Washington, it would do nothing to block them. It was confirmed to me in Europe at that time that this information had been passed on to Washington as soon as it became available. That again puts the mission of a high-

> level Canadian diplomat, Chester Ronning, to Hanoi in a different light. Ronning's mission to Hanoi was rapidly touted as a 'total failure' even though, according to unimpeachable reports, *Ronning himself did not see it that way* [our italics] (*New Republic,* July 16, 1966).

Ronning probably did not come back empty-handed, as is indicated by the very fact of the Sainteny mission. It would be rather remarkable for President de Gaulle, who had been negative on the possibility of negotiations early in May, to have sent so high-ranking a diplomat to Hanoi and Peking unless there had been some encouraging signs. Moreover, we must remember that neither of the missions could have gone unless Hanoi had allowed them to come in. In 1965, Hanoi had refused to allow a British Commonwealth mission to enter North Vietnam. Sainteny left Paris on June 17, and arrived in Peking a few days later. There he was reported as having had no talks with Chinese officials (*Le Monde,* June 24, 1966). He left for Hanoi via Shanghai, Hong Kong, and Vientiane. He arrived in Hanoi shortly after the bombings and left for Phnom Penh on July 8. In contrast to his reception in Peking, in Hanoi he had "friendly" conversations with Ho Chi Minh (*Le Monde,* July 9, 1966).

A further sign that prospects for negotiations had brightened was Secretary-General U Thant's three-point proposal for peace in Vietnam, made on June 20. Thant called for the cessation of bombing in North Vietnam, the scaling down of military actions in the South to achieve a cease-fire, and the opening of peace talks among all who are "actually fighting," which, of course, was meant to include the NLF. Thant, who reportedly feared that new American bombings were in the offing, labeled the Vietnam war one of the most barbarous in history (*NYT,* June 21, 1966). *The New York Times,* in an editorial, welcomed his proposal (June 22, 1966). Given U Thant's publicly expressed pessimism about negotiations in May, he must have gained the impression from diplomatic sources that Hanoi's attitude was softening. Indeed, on the same day (June 25) that it carried Max Frankel's article reviewing Washington's decision to bomb Hanoi and Haiphong, *The New York Times* reported that U Thant did not interpret Hanoi's reaction to American attempts to arrange peace talks as "an irrevocable rejection."

4. The Bombing of Hanoi and Haiphong

As these "signals" were beginning to emanate from Hanoi, however, President Johnson, on June 18, chose the moment to declare that "we must continue to raise the cost of aggression at its source." A week later, *The New York Times* and the *Wall Street Journal* reported that the U.S. was getting ready to bomb Hanoi and Haiphong. Controversy later arose because of the supposed "news leak" about the bombings. But in view of President Johnson's statement of June 18, it would be difficult to maintain that there had been a real disclosure of information. *The New York Times* (June 25) reported that the bombing had been planned for the spring but had been held up because of the political turmoil in South Vietnam. Allegedly because of the failure of the Ronning mission, the decision had been made to proceed with the plan. However, in view of the pattern of previous escalations described in this study, it appears unlikely that the political turmoil in South Vietnam had been a major factor in holding up the bombings. What appears more likely to us is that this particular timing was chosen to make certain that Hanoi would once again go back to its hard attitude.

On June 26, George Ball denied publicly that any decision to bomb Hanoi and Haiphong had been made.

On June 29, U.S. planes bombed the oil storage depots in the suburbs of Hanoi and Haiphong.

As in the past, Administration spokesmen argued that the latest escalation was calculated to hasten the ending of the war. North Vietnam's response was to order general mobilization of the entire population (*NYT*, July 18, 1966).

Throughout the world, including the United States, the Administration's action was condemned, most notably by Prime Minister Harold Wilson, who openly disassociated himself from the American action. James Reston noted: "There is now not a single major nation in the world that supports Mr. Johnson's latest adventure in Hanoi and Haiphong" (*NYT*, July 1, 1966).

The fighting did not abate; the spirit of the other side was not broken. Casualties continued to mount on all sides. Worst of all, as could have been predicted, escalation followed escalation. On July 30, U.S. planes bombed the demilitarized zone between North and South Vietnam. On August 3, American planes struck Haiphong for a third time, hitting targets only two miles northeast of the heart of the city. Hanoi charged indiscriminate bombing of residential quarters and factories (*San Francisco Chronicle,* August 3, 1966).

Whatever the military purpose and effect of the raids on Hanoi and Haiphong, there can be no doubt that they represent another major qualitative escalation of the war. The bombing of the two "sanctuaries" of Hanoi and Haiphong paved the way for the kind of total bombing envisaged by Bernard Fall (see below).

In the long run, however, the bombing of the demilitarized zone may have even more serious political consequences than the raids on Hanoi and Haiphong. On July 22, the Chinese announced that they no longer felt themselves bound by the Geneva Accords, that the demarcation line between North and South Vietnam had been broken, and that China would henceforth serve as a rear base area for the Vietnamese (*Peking People's Daily,* July 22, 1966). The Chinese statement was made in support of a declaration by Ho Chi Minh a few days earlier which had reiterated North Vietnam's four points and hence showed Hanoi's continued adherence to the key provisions of the Geneva Accords (*NYT,* July 18, 1966; for North Vietnam's four points, see Appendix B). The Defense Department justified the bombing of the demilitarized zone on military grounds. But while it had been well known for a long time that both South and North Vietnamese soldiers had been positioned in the demilitarized zone, one could not argue that it constituted a major route of infiltration. Moreover, the use of B-52's to saturate the area dramatized the political significance of the raids. One is forced to the conclusion that Washington's actions agreed with Peking's words that the Geneva Accords are no longer in effect.

In July, both Premier Ky and Chief of State Thieu spoke of launching an invasion of North Vietnam. Ky went further and called for a confrontation now with China. Despite the uproar created in Washington over his declaration, it is known that similar talk to this effect has been heard in American military circles in South Vietnam. If, as Robert Guillain indicates and other reports confirm, the Vietcong's hold is stronger than ever in the countryside and North Vietnamese infiltration is increasing (*Le Monde,* May 23, 1966), then the temptation to start an "Inchon" type landing in North Vietnam may be rising. If the Geneva Accords are no longer in effect, then neither is the 17th parallel. We shall have to wait for the future to see whether the declarations of Dean Rusk and George Ball that the United States is only fighting to preserve the "provisional boundaries and lines of demarcation" remain in effect. If not, then we shall undoubtedly hear once again that the destruction of the boundaries is the only reasonable road to peace.

Robert Guillain, the Far-Eastern correspondent of *Le Monde,* ended his series of five articles on Vietnam with a warning that a whole series of new escalations might ensue. He listed four possibilities:

(1) An attempt to isolate South Vietnam from the surrounding territory
(2) An invasion of North Vietnam
(3) Total bombardment of North Vietnam, including industrial sites and dike system [7]
(4) An attack on China, with a bombing of its industrial-military complex (*Le Monde,* May 26, 1966).

Given the interminable history of escalation, it would be idle to rule out any of these possibilities. During the March-May 1966 political crisis, Washington showed, by opposition to the Buddhist movement in the South and escalation of the bombing in the North, that it was determined to go on with the war. In late June, it again transmitted this same "signal" to Hanoi, not by words but by actions.

On his return from Moscow on July 30, 1966, U Thant said that the war in Vietnam was on the verge of erupting into a major war:

> "I don't want to go into specifics, but my feeling is that the fight might spill over the borders" (*NYT,* July 31).

That he gained this impression from his conferences with Soviet leaders is clear. Moreover, Prime Minister Harold Wilson's warnings to President Johnson against further escalation, likewise after a visit to Moscow, perhaps reflect the same source. Last spring, State Department officials, repeating Pres-

[7] Hanoi has already charged (in June 1966) that the United States had intensified its bombing of the dike system in recent weeks, at the time when the monsoon season was beginning. Hanoi alleged that there had been 500 attacks against the dikes between February and May (*Le Monde,* June 15, 1966).

ident Johnson's July 1964 statement that "We seek no wider war," tried to reassure China and North Vietnam that no American aggressive action against them was contemplated. But the ever-deepening "credibility gap" between what Washington says and does leaves little confidence in these statements.[8]

If the pattern of escalation continues, then a further internationalization of the war to the North (and elsewhere) and an even greater intensification of the war in the South seems likely. These were the fears of U Thant when he spoke of the dangers of the war spilling across borders and called it one of the most barbarous wars in history. We feel compelled to the conclusion that, during these last six months, as for the nine previous instances dealt with in the body of this study, Washington has again effectively blocked the chance of a peaceful settlement by its further escalation both in South and North Vietnam. One day after the bombing of Hanoi and Haiphong, James Reston, with evident anger, wrote that "The Johnson Administration said it was not seeking a military solution to the war and it is now obviously seeking precisely that" (*NYT*, July 1, 1966). We suggest that the predominant thrust of the Johnson Administration since its inception has been consistently toward a military solution. What is even more alarming, however, are the prospects that such a military solution will bring about a much wider war than at present and confront the people of Vietnam with the tragedy of total destruction.

Bernard Fall has written:

> ". . . As in Korea the Vietnam war is now likely to ride the upswing of the blood-drenched roller coaster into the annihilation of industries, flood control and irrigation dams, and cities and villages—for, after all, when all of North Vietnam will supply the Vietcong and the infiltrated divisions with the help of massive coolie labor, *people* must become a strategic target. And they will. Never fear, they will" (*New Republic*, July 16, 1966).

A basic change in America's present policy in Vietnam can still prevent the fulfillment of this agonized prediction.

[8] On the matter of news management, see the criticisms by leading American newsmen in South Vietnam against the Pentagon's news policies (*San Francisco Chronicle*, August 2, 1966).

AFTERWORD:

Origin of the Citizens' White Paper

Just a year ago, news of North Vietnamese overtures for negotiations finally reached the American public. Until that fall of 1965, it was widely accepted in this country that our actions in Vietnam were against an enemy that refused every opportunity to negotiate. If the reports of peace feelers given out by Eric Sevareid, and later by U Thant himself, were accurate, the American people had been misled. The existence of these overtures, first denied and then admitted by our State Department, came as a shock to many Americans. The revelations created what came to be known as the "credibility crisis" for the Johnson Administration. The moves and countermoves that followed as the Administration struggled to close the credibility gap only added to the public's confusion.

Like others throughout the country, a group in St. Louis, consisting largely of professors at Washington University, were baffled by the admissions and denials issuing from Washington. For more than a year, this group had been meeting informally as the Foreign Policy Roundtable to share facts and opinions on foreign affairs. While no member of the group was professionally expert on Vietnam, all of the members were at a particular advantage in having easy access to one of the nation's great newspapers.

The St. Louis *Post-Dispatch* has for several years led in coverage of the Vietnam war. With a Washington staff, including Richard Dudman and James Deakin, making great efforts to follow American policy as it developed and visiting Vietnam from time to time, and Donald Grant, providing the finest reports available from the United Nations, the *Post-Dispatch* has kept St. Louis the best informed of cities. When Robert Lasch of the *Post-Dispatch* received the Pulitzer Prize for his editorials on Vietnam, it could be seen in part as made possible by the work of those reporters in Washington and in the United Nations. Their daily reports, shared by all St. Louisans, convinced the Foreign Policy Roundtable that much could be learned from a careful assembling of the record of events taking place in Vietnam.

Another advantage possessed by the group was the special background of several of the Roundtable participants. Among the group were Dan I. Bolef, Barry Commoner, Peter Gaspar, and Daniel H. Kohl, all scientists with long experience in promoting public understanding of complex issues, and Bernard S. Baumrin, a philosopher. Time and again, these people had been turned to by groups of laymen confused by statements from government and elsewhere on the effects of fallout, the damage of nuclear war, the dangers of air pollutants, and similar public issues. As a result, St. Louis, with its Committee on Nuclear Information, became the home of the science "information" movement, which now has groups in many cities across the country. These committees, together with the journal *Scientist and Citizen*, published by the St. Louis group, have been termed "a new social invention" by anthropologist Margaret Mead.

Over the years, these scientists worked to communicate their knowledge of scientifically complicated and politically controversial issues to fellow citizens, and out of that developed a view of the expert's role in society. The scientist, they believe, has a special responsibility—to present facts to the public. He should not mix his personal convictions with the facts, nor should he cloak his political beliefs in the role of scientific expertise.

The importance of this approach was borne out in experience with the public. Citizens at large appreciated the work of scientists in providing needed information. They recognized the efforts of the scientist to separate facts from opinions and came to trust and utilize the information provided.

With this experience, members of the Foreign Policy Roundtable saw the daily turns of U.S. policy in Vietnam as yet another area where they and the public badly needed the help of experts. As in the science information movement, the expert was not needed to tell the citizens what to conclude, but rather to ferret out the facts and present them in an understandable manner. After that, the expert and the nonexpert are on the same footing—each is a citizen with one vote; the conclusions of each will emerge from the interplay of the facts with his own morality, political preferences, and set of priorities. In short, it was felt that the public needed the help of experts in order to provide the raw material for the functioning of the democratic process.

For these reasons, the faculty Roundtable sought out their colleagues in history. Historians, it was thought, were especially equipped with the knowledge and techniques to gather information on Vietnam and assemble it in the context of events developing in time.

Quite by chance, Barry Commoner, of the St. Louis group, met Carl E. Schorske, historian, of the University of California at Berkeley. Dr. Schorske's enthusiasm for a factual presentation of the subject of negotiations in Vietnam led him to other colleagues on the Berkeley faculty, the present authors. Franz Schurmann, Reginald Zelnik, and Peter Dale Scott were already at work as members of the Faculty Peace Committee at Berkeley on a series of analyses of the war in Vietnam. Several had already been broadcasted by Pacifica Foundation's radio station KPFA. The plea from St. Louis and the offer of assistance in a larger project encouraged the Berkeley scholars to attempt a fuller examination of the subject of negotiations. Shortly after, a substantial financial contribution came from the Inter-University Committee for Debate on Foreign Policy.

This study represents the best efforts of these scholars at the unusual task of assembling a record of extremely contemporary events. Normally, the historian would have the benefit of many years' perspective on the events he studied, as well as access to important documents in the archives of government. The authors of this history make much of these restrictions.

Citing the gravity of the public record as it now stands, they have asked that responsible political leaders correct their version where it may be in error. Twenty-nine prominent citizens have told the President that in their view the weight of evidence in this assessment of the public record demands clarification or refutation by the government.

Evidence from available sources has been assembled, a preliminary assessment of the record has been taken, and both have been transmitted to the leadership in Washington. No response has been forthcoming from responsible officials, and this limited record must stand for future historians and for the public. With the publication of this book, the evidence is now presented to a wider audience, and we have great faith that they will obtain the necessary answers.

The first steps in this process have been taken. Senator Vance Hartke of Indiana gave each of his colleagues in the Senate a copy of the study and then presented a summary of the White Paper in a speech to the Senate on June 30, 1966.

Pointing to the bombing of Hanoi and Haiphong, which had just taken place, Senator Hartke drew on the White Paper:

> . . . this historical study of facts and events, including some peace proposals which did not come to light until weeks or months later, brings to attention an apparent pattern of action which I fear is once more being repeated.
> . . . the fact is inescapable that, in the juxtaposition of events on the peace front and on the military front, time and time again just as there appeared some possibility of movement toward a negotiated reduction of the conflict, military escalation has been tightened another notch.

Senator Hartke was the first to take up the evidence assembled in the White Paper. Others have followed him, in the Senate and elsewhere. A number of newspapers followed presentation of the White Paper material with a call for explanation by the government. The *Baltimore Sun* editorialized:

> The paper suggests . . . that there is a disturbing pattern of repeated escalation of United States military operations in Vietnam in the face of possible opportunities for peace negotiations.
> If the authors of the paper are wrong, they should be refuted by evidence, as they themselves say (*Baltimore Sun*, Monday, June 27, 1966).

A similar request addressed to the Administration came from Senator William Fulbright to Under-Secretary of State George Ball in hearings before the Senate Foreign Relations Committee. Ball replied that military actions were not timed to interfere with political maneuvers, and that the thesis of the White Paper was "just not true" (St. Louis *Post-Dispatch*, June 30, 1966).

However, with the exception of this offhand remark by Mr. Ball, no reply has been made by the White House or others in the Administration to the evidence assembled in *The Politics of Escalation in Vietnam*. Neither have the signers of the letter of transmittal to the President received a response. Perhaps the editor of *The Nation* best expressed the view of all involved in the Citizens' White Paper when he wrote:

> Its immediate impact will be mainly on thoughtful Americans, who have been notably deficient in their influence on this Administration. This effort, however, differs from previous ones in that it is not so much a remonstrance as a marshaling of evidence that, in time, can hardly fail to raise questions (*The Nation*, July 11, 1966).

We hope that thoughtful Americans will continue their response to the questions raised by this book.

LINDSAY MATTISON
St. Louis
August 1966

APPENDIX A:

The Fourteen Points of the United States

(The following text was published in the Department of State *Bulletin* of January 24, 1966, page 116.)

U. S. Contributions to the Basket of Peace[1]

The following statements are on the public record about elements which the U.S. believes can go into peace in Southeast Asia:

1. The Geneva Agreements of 1954 and 1962 are an adequate basis for peace in Southeast Asia;
2. We would welcome a conference on Southeast Asia or on any part thereof;
3. We would welcome "negotiations without preconditions" as the 17 nations put it;
4. We would welcome unconditional discussions as President Johnson put it;
5. A cessation of hostilities could be the first order of business at a conference or could be the subject of preliminary discussions;
6. Hanoi's four points could be discussed along with other points which others might wish to propose;
7. We want no U.S. bases in Southeast Asia;
8. We do not desire to retain U.S. troops in South Vietnam after peace is assured;
9. We support free elections in South Vietnam to give the South Vietnamese a government of their own choice;
10. The question of reunification of Vietnam should be determined by the Vietnamese through their own free decision;

[1] The following covering statement and the 14 numbered paragraphs were released separately by the Department of State on January 7 (press release 4) under the heading "United States Official Position on Vietnam."

11. The countries of Southeast Asia can be nonaligned or neutral if that be their option:
12. We would much prefer to use our resources for the economic reconstruction of Southeast Asia than in war. If there is peace, North Vietnam could participate in a regional effort to which we would be prepared to contribute at least one billion dollars;
13. The President has said [2] "The Vietcong would not have difficulty being represented and having their views represented if for a moment Hanoi decided she wanted to cease aggression. I don't think that would be an insurmountable problem."
14. We have said publicly and privately that we could stop the bombing of North Vietnam as a step toward peace although there has not been the slightest hint or suggestion from the other side as to what they would do if the bombing stopped.

In other words, we have put everything into the basket of peace except the surrender of South Vietnam.

[2] At a press conference on July 28, 1965.

APPENDIX B:

The Four Points of North Vietnam

(The following text of Premier Pham Van Dong's speech of April 8, 1965, was issued by the Consulate General of the Democratic Republic of Vietnam, New Delhi: in *Vietnam,* Vol. V, No. 70 (July 20, 1965), p. 3)

Basis of a Correct Solution to the Vietnam Problem

The unswerving policy of the Government of the Democratic Republic of Vietnam to strictly respect the Geneva Agreements on Vietnam, and to correctly implement their basic provisions is embodied in the following points:

1. Recognition of the basic national rights of the Vietnamese people: Peace, independence, sovereignty, unity and territorial integrity. According to the Geneva Agreements, the U.S. government must withdraw from South Vietnam all U.S. troops, military personnel and weapons of all kinds, dismantle all U.S. military bases there, cancel its 'military alliance' with South Vietnam. It must end its policy of intervention and aggression in South Vietnam. According to the Geneva Agreements, the U.S. Government must stop its acts of war against North Vietnam: completely cease all encroachments on the territory and sovereignty of the Democratic Republic of Vietnam.

2. Pending the peaceful reunification of Vietnam, while Vietnam is still temporarily divided into two zones, the military provisions of the 1954 Geneva Agreements on Vietnam must be strictly respected: the two zones must refrain from joining any military alliance with foreign countries, there must be no foreign military bases, troops and military personnel in their respective territories.

3. The internal affairs of South Vietnam must be settled by the South Vietnamese people themselves, in accordance with the program of the South Vietnam National Front for Liberation, without any foreign interference.

4. The peaceful reunification of Vietnam is to be settled by the Vietnamese people in both zones themselves, without any foreign interference.

This stand unquestionably enjoys the approval and support of all peace and justice loving governments and people in the world.

The Government of the Democratic Republic of Vietnam is of the view that the above-expounded stand is the basis for the soundest political settlement of the Vietnam problem. If this basis is recognized, favorable conditions will be created for the peaceful settlement of the Vietnam problem and it will be possible to consider the reconvening of an international conference along the pattern of the 1954 Geneva Conference on Vietnam.

APPENDIX C:

Letter of Transmittal to President Johnson (June 22, 1966)

The Honorable Lyndon B. Johnson
The White House
Washington, D. C.

Dear Mr. President:

This nation, and the world, are attempting to negotiate a fateful passage in history. We are desperately trying to learn how to establish peace in the world in the face of existing differences in ideology, deep national aspirations, and continuing injustice—under the constant threat of a nuclear war.

Our hopes for world peace, and our fears of world disaster, are centered at this time on Vietnam. Here, for over five years, this nation has committed its political power, its military force, and the lives of its youth, to a struggle which each day becomes less clear in its purpose, more uncertain in its outcome, and more dangerous in its approach to the ultimate disaster of nuclear war.

You, the United States Government, and Americans generally have looked for ways to end this unhappy war. The search has been extraordinarily difficult. Profoundly discouraging, too, has been the fact that the numerous efforts to find a path to peace in Vietnam have not only failed in themselves, but that we have been unable to understand these failures and to learn from them how we might succeed.

Much of our policy in Vietnam has been based on the historical analogy of our encounter with Nazism and Stalinism, an experience of ten to thirty years ago. A group of historians has now examined a past more recent and more relevant: the history of American involvement in Vietnam itself since 1963. Their findings are presented in the attached study.

The historians disclose a disturbing pattern of connections between negotiations and escalation, between political opportunities to approach peace and military actions that widen the war. The authors are well aware that, working only from the public record, their facts are incomplete and their perspective partial. Yet, the recent pattern they discern in the history of United States policy is of such grave import that we believe it to merit your serious attention: if wrong, to be refuted by evidence; if right, to become a guide to policy. The time has come, we believe, to seek a new perspective and to learn from our actual experience in Vietnam why we have thus far failed to achieve peace. We believe that the enclosed document may shed light on our past failures and thus open a new perspective toward peace. We urgently submit this document to your attention, and through you, to the attention of the American people.

Respectfully,

Charles A. Bane
John C. Bennett
Eugene Carson Blake
Robert McAfee Brown
Benjamin J. Buttenwieser
Benton R. Cancell
Grenville Clark
Barry Commoner
Clifford J. Durr
William Eastlake
Marriner S. Eccles
Robert C. Garretson
Maxwell Geismar
J. W. Gitt
Patrick E. Gorman
Abraham J. Heschel
Robert M. Hutchins
Arnold Kaufman
Martin Luther King
Edward Lamb
Irving F. Laucks
David Livingston
Arno J. Mayer
James G. Patton
B. T. Rocca, Sr.
Frank Rosenblum
Carl Schorske
Jacob J. Weinstein
C. Vann Woodward

IDENTIFICATION OF SIGNERS

(Organizational or institutional affiliation, where listed, is for identification only)

Charles A. Bane
Attorney, Chicago

John C. Bennett
President, Union Theological Seminary

Eugene Carson Blake
General Secretary-Elect, World Council of Churches

Robert McAfee Brown
Professor, Stanford University

Benjamin J. Buttenwieser
New York City

Benton R. Cancell
San Francisco

Grenville Clark
Lawyer and author, New York City

Barry Commoner
Professor of Botany, Washington University

Clifford J. Durr
Attorney, Montgomery

William Eastlake
Author

Marriner S. Eccles
Salt Lake City

Robert C. Garretson
Cleveland

Maxwell Geismar
Historian, critic of U.S. Literature

J. W. Gitt
York, Pennsylvania

Patrick E. Gorman
Secretary-Treasurer, Amalgamated Meatcutters and Butcher Workmen of North America, AFL-CIO

Abraham J. Heschel
Professor, Jewish Theological Seminary of America

Robert M. Hutchins
Santa Barbara

Arnold Kaufman
Professor of Philosophy, University of Michigan

Martin Luther King
Southern Christian Leadership Conference

Edward Lamb
President, Seilon, Inc., Lamb Industries, Inc., Toledo

Irving F. Laucks
Santa Barbara

David Livingston
President, District 65, Retail Workers Department Store Union, AFL-CIO

Arno J. Mayer
Professor of History, Princeton University

James G. Patton
Denver

B. T. Rocca, Sr.
Honorary Chairman of the Board, Pacific Vegetable Oil Corp., San Francisco

Frank Rosenblum
General Secretary-Treasurer, Amalgamated Clothing Workers of America, AFL-CIO

Carl Schorske
Professor of History, University of California, Berkeley

Jacob J. Weinstein
President, Central Conference of American Rabbis

C. Vann Woodward
Professor of History, Yale University

INDEX